SURVIVING CATASTROPHE

Lessons Learned from the Wedgwood Shooting

Dr. Al Meredith

Surviving Catastrophe: Lessons Learned from the Wedgwood Shooting

Copyright © 2019 by Dr. Al Meredith

Author: Dr. Al Meredith
Author assistant: Kay Meredith
Publishing assistant: Josh Meredith
Manuscript editor: Amy McMullin
Format editor: Phil McMullin
Cover design: Bill Stahler

www.facebook.com/BroAlMeredith/

PRINTED IN THE UNITED STATES OF AMERICA.

"This will be written for the generation to come,
That a people yet to be created may praise the Lord."

PSALM 102:18

Dedicated to:

The Glory of Christ alone, our sovereign Lord and King

My wife, Kay, who is my soulmate and fellow traveller on this journey called life

CONTENTS

FORWARD

The Puritans once used the phrase "Blind Afflictions" to refer to people who had suffered greatly but never learned any lessons from their adversities. Whether through intellectual or spiritual laziness, or some sense of fatalism, they simply suffered purposelessly.

King David transparently confessed, "Before I was afflicted I went astray, But now I keep Your word" (Psalm 119:67). Not all afflictions fall under the category of chastening, but something can be learned from every trial.

This book contains just a few of the many lessons we at Wedgwood Baptist Church have gleaned from the mass shooting we experienced that dark night 20 years ago.

It is my prayer that what God has taught us can be of comfort and aid to others, no matter what the affliction. If we can be of any help or comfort to "those who are in any trouble with the comfort with which we ourselves are comforted by God" (2 Corinthians 1:4), then our trials were not in vain.

"And our hope for you is steadfast, because we know that as you are partakers of the sufferings, so also you will partake of the consolation" (2 Corinthians 1:7).

Dr. Al Meredith
Former Senior Pastor of Wedgwood Baptist Church
Fort Worth, Texas
July 15, 2019

INTRODUCTION

"THE GURU OF GRIEF"

It had happened once again. A crazed gunman had entered a church on a Sunday morning and began opening fire on a helpless congregation. This time 26 were murdered and 20 more were wounded by the bullet.

Soon, my phone began ringing insistently. First, our local newspaper rang, and then four of the major networks. National Public Radio followed. Finally, the Christian networks called. All were asking for interviews from the Pastor who had been through it in his own church.

From 9/11 to Sandy Hook to Virginia Tech...Charleston, South Carolina...Aurora, Colorado...Maryville, Illinois...and now Sutherland Springs, Texas.

When gun violence strikes shockingly, where you least expect it, call Pastor Meredith. Little wonder I had begun to feel like "The Guru of Grief."

"What are these people going through, Pastor?"

"What can they expect next?"

"What do you say when people ask why God allows such terrible things to happen to His people?"

"Where is God in all of this?"

"Can you give hope to these people?"

OUR STORY

It was September 15, 1999, a Wednesday evening. Our worship center was packed with nearly 500 young teens. It was "See You at the Pole" day across the nation. Students would gather around the flagpole at their various campuses, on their own initiative, to pray for their schools before classes began.

This particular evening, Wedgwood Baptist Church in Fort Worth, Texas, was hosting a "Saw You at the Pole" rally. We had invited a dozen or so other churches to join us. Many of these were churches that went to Youth Camp with us the previous summer. The Praise Band from camp was leading us in worship. It was an exciting time.

Shortly after the music began, a man no one had ever known, walked into the church smoking a cigarette and armed with approximately 200 rounds of ammunition and a pipe bomb. He asked, "Where is that [expletive] prayer meeting?"

Then he began firing. Down the hall he went, shooting his way into the worship center.

Before he was finished, seven people were wounded, and seven more young people were murdered. Then, he turned the gun on himself, and the carnage stopped.

I wasn't even there when it happened. (I will talk about False, or Survivor, Guilt later.)

I had spent the week before in my hometown in Michigan attending to my dying mother. My sisters and I had literally sung her into Heaven. On Monday, I preached her funeral. On Tuesday, we cleaned out my childhood home and took care of the affairs of my older sister. On Wednesday, I flew back to Fort Worth. I remember sitting on the dock on the beautiful St. Clair River thinking,

"When I get back to Fort Worth, I am going to have to take some time to process this grief."

I had asked one of our many seminary students to lead Prayer Meeting for me, but I was planning to be at the rally. Circumstances, however, made me a few minutes late. As I was still at the dinner table, the phone rang, and one of my deacons asked if I knew anything about a shooting at the church.

I laughed skeptically and said it must be a wild rumor or I would have heard. No sooner had I hung up than the phone rang again. It was the religion reporter from the Star-Telegram.

"Pastor Al. There's been a shooting at your church!"

I hung up without responding, jumped into my car, and made the normal five-minute drive in less than three.

I was stopped about a block away, and the scene looked to me like a beehive. A number of helicopters were flying overhead. Cars with flashing blue and red lights from every law enforcement and first responder agency in the county were there.

The first thing I saw as I ran to the scene was our Staff Counselor, Kevin Galey, on the ground as medics were giving him plasma to replace the blood he was losing.

The wail of teenagers crying, screaming bewilderedly filled the air. Then, my Youth Pastor, Jay Fannin, came running and collapsed in my arms.

"How many, Jay?" I asked. "Who's been shot?"

He then began to tell me the ones he knew for sure.

Teenagers. I wondered how I was going to inform their unspeakably heartbroken parents.

Seminary students. Lives cut off before they could begin to make their mark for the Kingdom.

Sydney. Our Children's Choir Director.

But before we could do or say anything, the police began to ask for help. I needed to help round up all the youth and lead them across the street to the elementary school for questioning and de-briefing.

Parents who were insisting on seeing their children, in gripping panic that their child might be counted among the casualties, needed to be calmed somehow to allow the officers to do their work.

Sobbing youth, adults, and fellow church members clung to one another and formed spontaneous prayer groups. Children who had fled their mid-week activities needed to be consoled and reunited with their parents.

That night was, and still is, a blur.

I accompanied hundreds of shell-shocked young people downtown to police headquarters for individual questioning, praying with them, hearing the shocking stories of gunfire in the worship center, blood on the floor, an explosion, and shrapnel raining down.

Most of them thought it was a skit. It was only five months earlier that the shooting at Columbine High School had occurred near Denver, Colorado. As our gunman paced back and forth cursing, students remembering Cassie Bernall popped up from beneath the pews declaring, "I believe in God!" Then they would duck back down as the shooter grew more and more frustrated and angry.

After helping to organize the survivors, I began to visit the hospitals where the wounded were being treated. Tom Law, our Tarrant Baptist Association's Director of Missions, drove me around through the night. I prayed with the wounded and their parents.

I made three trips to the morgue to help shocked loved ones identify their children or their spouse.

We wept. We prayed. We listened. We hugged, and we cried some more.

I got back to the church around daybreak and Police Chief Ralph Mendoza told me a press conference had been scheduled for 7 am on the corner of the street outside the church. They spent about ten minutes trying to coach me on how to respond to the Press.

I cannot remember anything they said.

For several blocks around our church, the streets were blocked with satellite trucks from around the nation, each seeking to report back to their communities the horrifying story.

The Chief gave a brief description of what had happened in a monotone voice, and then he introduced me...

A nurse, whom I later found out had helped in the Oklahoma City bombing, had handed me a note saying, "This verse may help you."

It was Habakkuk 3:17-19. This is one of my favorite verses of Scripture. My wife, Kay, even cross-stitched it and framed it to hang in my office.

"Though the fig tree may not blossom,
Nor fruit be on the vines;
Though the labor of the olive may fail,
And the fields yield no food;
Though the flock be cut off from the fold,
And there be no herd in the stalls—
Yet I will rejoice in the Lord,
I will joy in the God of my salvation.
The Lord God is my strength;
He will make my feet like deer's feet,
And He will make me walk on my high hills."

So, I explained that though we as a church were broken over the events of the night before, we were not crushed. Should we sing God's praises only on the good days and not on the bad?

The first question someone asked me was, "Where was God in all of this?"

Good question. Fine question. Deep question.

The answer God gave me that morning was this:

"God is exactly where He has always been—on His throne. He is the sovereign Lord of the Universe, and He is not up for reelection. He was not on vacation."

"He is a parent who knows what it is like to see His only Son cruelly beaten and murdered, and He weeps with us over these tragic events. He knows what we are going through."

"He is in control, and He cares deeply for each one of us!"

And then the press conference was closed, and I finally went home. But the real action was only about to begin.

This book is about the aftermath of those horrific, violent events.

Denominational leaders told me that most churches break up after traumatic events of this order. The trauma is too deep; the emotional and spiritual carnage is too overwhelming to overcome. The guilt, pain, resentment, and sorrow are so overwhelming that most churches just do not survive.

Wedgwood did not just survive; we actually grew by 50 percent in the next five years. We grew closer to one another and to the Lord. Our worship became more intense than ever. Our opportunities for outreach and missions multiplied. We found favor not only in our own community but also around the world.

You will likely never be involved in a mass shooting. But every one of us goes through times of deep, traumatic loss and grief.

A loved one dies. A marriage falls apart. The diagnosis is deadly. A beloved child ends up in jail or on drugs. A car crash disables for months, years, or for life. The sudden unexpected death of a loved one leaves us as emotional cripples.

Organizations, be they churches or businesses or schools, are rocked by charges of abuse, funds absconded, moral failures of trusted leaders.

How does one respond to all of this?

One of the growth industries in our nation is Security measures. These "Sheepdog Ministries" are good when the emphasis is on preparation, not paranoia. As leaders, we are responsible to do all we reasonably can to make our people safe from harm.

But those ministries deal with what is to be done *before* or *during* the shooting.

This book is primarily about how to respond *after* the shooting stops, after the darkness descends, once the shock wears off and you become "Yesterday's News."

Can we survive—even thrive—in the aftermath of catastrophic events? Can God really turn all things together for our good (Romans 8:28)?

The people of Wedgwood Baptist Church and I want to give a resounding affirmative to all these questions and more.

OUR MARTYRS

Sydney Browning

Sydney had come to Fort Worth from Phoenix, Arizona, to attend Southwestern Baptist Theological Seminary. After graduation, she taught high school in the inner city at one of our alternative schools. It was basically the last chance for troublesome students. Twice, she had been voted Outstanding Teacher of the Year.

Sydney had discussed with her students at various times what they would do if a shooter came into their school in a manner like Columbine. In her typical humorous way, she joked that she hoped he would shoot her and not them because she was the only one in the room with health insurance!

Around this time, Sydney had phoned her mother about having dreams of a shooting. Her mother had also had similar dreams. They both thought that if it ever happened, it would be at her inner-city school, not in her suburban church.

Sydney was the Director of our Children's Choir at Wedgwood and was beloved by all. Young and old alike loved her for the way she sang and played and laughed so easily. She was one of the very active members of our Singles Ministry. She loved her pastor enough to hold him accountable, with tears in her eyes, when he got off base.

She was where she was supposed to be, sitting in the church foyer, talking with friends, and waiting for choir practice to begin.

When the gunman walked in, Sydney became the first fatality.

I miss her still.

Kim Jones

Kim was a bright and bubbly graduate of Texas Christian University. She had just begun attending Southwestern Baptist Theological Seminary that September. Although raised in a Christian home, she had only recently totally surrendered her life to Christ. Her father was a supervisor in the oil industry in Saudi Arabia, and Kim had spent the previous summer as Youth Minister in the Protestant Church on the compound. She had one of the most infectious smiles I have ever seen.

I have seen a video of her sharing with the teens in her youth group. She had her backpack and talked about backpacking across Europe. As exciting as that journey was for her, she shared how temporary her backpack was, how transient it was to sleep in hostels and cheap hotels, and how she looked forward to the day when she could drop her backpack on the floor of her home and lie down on her warm, cozy bed. She would be home at last!

In the same way, she explained, this present world is as temporary as her backpack. Our lives may be filled with adventures and joy, but these are only fleeting experiences. And, they are nothing compared to the joy that will be ours when we finally get "Home" to Heaven.

Her mother explained that, if we asked who wanted to go to Heaven today, Kim's hand would be the first one raised.

Kim was on her way to prayer meeting that evening when she heard the music in the worship center. She was absolutely addicted to praise and worship, so she slipped into the back row. In a matter of minutes, she was translated from the back row of our sanctuary to the front row of God's Worship Center.

Kim had a deep desire to share her testimony with all of her sorority sisters at Texas Christian University. As a result of her death at the shooting, she fulfilled that dream a hundred times over.

I long to join her in song one day soon.

Shawn Brown

Shawn Brown had been married to his college sweetheart, Kathy Jo, for 22 months. He was a student at Southwestern Baptist Theological Seminary preparing to be a Youth Minister. They were leaders in our preteen ministry, and he was at the concert to help with crowd control and any other thing that was needed.

Both Shawn and Kathy Jo were blessed with servant hearts.

Shawn had played baseball for Howard Payne University and loved Christian rap music and driving his pickup truck across the west Texas plains.

When he heard the shooting in the hallway, he immediately went out the back of the sanctuary and across the hall into the office to call for help. Then, he returned to the worship center to see how he could help.

The sanctuary was darkened for the concert, so when he opened the door, the sunlight in the hallway from the west windows made him a perfect profile.

The gunman shot him immediately, and he died in the hallway.

Nobody was so eager to be used of God in service to His Kingdom than Shawn Brown. His smiling face, servant's spirit, positive attitude, and joyful personality are terribly missed by all who knew and loved him.

Cassie Griffin

Cassie Griffin was a 14-year-old student at North Crowley High School where she played clarinet in the band. She was a "people magnet." The only one she loved more than other people was her Savior, Jesus Christ.

She was genuinely excited for the Saw You at the Pole rally. She had been there at her school flagpole that morning along with friends she had invited in the last several weeks.

One of her friends had not been able to make it that morning, so later in the day, Cassie wrote to her friend:

"I was crying this morning for you and every other non-Christian in our school. It's just that I love you so much, I don't want you to go to hell. I've been praying for you a lot. I love you soooo much."

She had invited a number of her friends over for supper that evening, so the car was packed as her mother drove them to the rally.

Cassie was a deeply devoted Christ-follower. Her life's motto was "FROG": Fully Rely On God. Her bedroom at home was filled with frog stuffed animals, pictures, and figurines.

She was sitting in the second row, as Charles Wesley describes, "lost in wonder, love and praise." She was singing her heart out when a bullet from a crazed gunman ushered her into eternity where the praise will never end.

A life so full of promise and joy was not ended. It was merely translated to a higher level.

But that does not mean her absence does not give us deep pain and sorrow.

Kristi Beckel

Kristi was an honor student at Bethesda Christian School where she also played volleyball and basketball. She had just begun getting involved in Wedgwood's Youth Ministry and was at school for the morning prayer time at the flagpole with her friends. Volleyball practice had been cancelled, so she was able to join her new friends in praise at the rally as the praise band from camp, "Forty Days," led them.

As an athlete, Kristi specialized in setting her teammates up, whether as a setter in volleyball or a point guard in basketball. She felt successful when she helped others score.

Kristi's heart continued to beat after she was shot. Later that night, it was apparent to the doctors that Kristi was not going to recover. Her brain activity was zero. And so, after heart-wrenching prayer, her parents allowed the doctors to remove life support so that the functioning parts of her body, now emptied of her soul and spirit, might be donated to others. Scores of other patients benefited from her eyes, kidneys, liver, skin, and so forth. It was indeed fitting that Kristi, who helped others in her brief life, would do so in her death as well.

Joey Ennis

Joey Ennis was a point guard on the ninth-grade basketball team at Brewer High School in northwest Fort Worth. He was newly involved in the youth group of First Baptist Church of White Settlement and was expressing interest in baptism as a sign of his newfound faith in Christ.

He was devoted to his single-parent mother and loved basketball, board games, and watching videos with her. Unlike many teens, Joey often told his mother how much he loved and appreciated her.

He had promised his cousin he would go with him to the rally at Wedgwood, but he later changed his mind and made other plans. In an effort to teach him to keep his commitments, his mother insisted that he spend the evening with his cousin, whether at the concert or at home.

They chose to go with their youth group.

The last song he listened to on the church van was the old Gospel song, "I'll Fly Away." That night, the song became reality.

Justin "Steggy" Ray

Justin Ray, known as "Steggy" by his friends, was a senior at Cassata High School, but he was also involved in the media technology program at nearby Southwest High School. Tim Hood was the director of that program and also served as the "sound man" at Wedgwood. Steggy helped him there and also got involved with the youth group. That afternoon, he assisted Tim and the band in setting up their sound system.

He was told he was not needed for the rally, but he chose to stay and help in any manner he could. Steggy was given the assignment of video recording the rally. He returned home for supper. While there, he called his grandmother to apologize for missing their dinner date that night and rescheduled it. Telling both his mother and grandmother he loved them, he hurried back to Wedgwood to his place in the balcony to video the meeting.

When the shooting started, Steggy, like so many others, thought the gunshots were part of a skit. To get a better view, he walked down from the balcony to the floor of the sanctuary.

It was then that a bullet from a man he had never met took his life.

Having just begun his walk of faith with Christ, he was translated into the presence of the King.

Larry Gene Ashbrook

The gunman, Larry Gene Ashbrook, also died that night from a self-inflicted wound.

No answer to the ever-present "Why?" question has ever been convincingly proffered. As far as we know, no one affiliated with Wedgwood had ever met or come in conflict with him. This was a particular blessing since there was no one to hold any guilt or blame for the tragedy, humanly speaking, except the shooter himself.

Strangely enough, Ashbrook had been raised in a church-going home. As a youth, he had been part of his pastor's "Preacher-boy Class," travelling with him to denominational rallies and meetings and sharing his testimony. But even then, he tended to be a bit of a loner.

He enlisted for a while in the Navy, but his psychological issues and misanthropy led to a dishonorable discharge.

His mother had died several years prior, and three months before the shooting, his father, with whom he lived, passed away. Ashbrook's paranoia and schizophrenia ramped up in the ensuing months. He wrote several letters to the Fort Worth Chief of Police complaining about psychological harassment from the CIA. Perhaps he was fearful that the family home he lived in would be sold out from under him and he would be forced into the ranks of the homeless.

As his fear and anger grew with each passing day, it finally culminated on the fateful day of September 15, 1999. He set about destroying the house: he poured concrete down the toilets, took a claw hammer to the sheetrock, upended the furniture, destroyed the pictures, and even poisoned the fruit trees on the front lawn.

Then, he got into his car and drove the nine miles to Wedgwood Baptist Church, armed with more than two hundred rounds of ammunition, two handguns, and a pipe bomb. He was bent on death and destruction.

After opening fire in the hallway, Ashbrook entered the back of the worship center, firing sporadically and cursing Christians in general and Baptists in particular.

Pacing back and forth across the back of the auditorium, it became increasingly clear that he was growing ever angrier. No one seemed to be taking him seriously. Everyone assumed it was just a skit. That it was actually a horrible assault upon teenagers in a church was a thought too heinous to consider.

So, what brought it all to an end? The facts are almost too surreal to believe.

Seated four or five rows from the back was a 19-year-old young man named Jeremiah Neitz.

Jeremiah grew up in a single-parent home. His mother held several jobs just to keep food on the table. In many ways, he was forced to raise himself.

While in middle school, he became friends with some kids from a nearby church, Southwayside Baptist Church. There he learned about God's love for him and of Christ who died for his sins. He became a Christ-follower.

But once in high school, he got caught up in the wrong crowd. Alcohol and drugs soon led him to drop out of school.

His life had fallen completely apart when, several months before the shooting, he lost his job and his girlfriend announced she was expecting a baby. His mother was unable to help; his "thug" friends were unwilling. In desperation, he turned to the God he had abandoned.

Jeremiah felt in his heart the need to go back to Southwayside and start over. Reluctantly and fearful he would be rejected by the youth, he returned on a Wednesday night and was immediately embraced and accepted by those who could still recognize this red-headed, studded, six-foot-two 19-year-old.

The Youth Minister took Jeremiah under his wing and began to disciple him. And so it was that their group found themselves at the rally that fateful night.

As Jeremiah hid beneath the pew, he wondered, like the others, whether or not it was just a skit. But then his jeans began to get soaked from the blood of the wounded and dying. Suddenly, he got up from under the pew and began to rock back and forth praying, "Oh God, make it stop!" All the while, his Youth Minister was pulling on his pant leg, pleading with him to take cover.

Then, there was a pause in the shooting as the gunman reloaded. At that time, Jeremiah boldly confronted the shooter:

"Sir," he said. "I know what you need. You need Jesus Christ in your life."

Ashbrook just cursed and racked his handgun.

To which Jeremiah responded, holding his arms wide defenselessly.

"Ok. Go ahead and shoot me. I know where I am going when I die. Do you know where you are going?"

What happened next is inexplicable. It is the author's opinion that the spiritual darkness that had taken over Ashbrook's heart and mind, confronted by such bold truth, fled. Suddenly, he realized where he was and what he was doing, and, confronted by that unthinkable truth, he turned the gun upon himself and the carnage was ended.

Other Victims

The list of the other victims that night is a sad and lengthy one.

Wounded in the shooting were Kevin Galey, the Staff Counselor of Wedgwood.

Jeff Laster, a student at Southwestern and a Church Custodian, took several bullets to the abdomen.

Justin Laird was celebrating his sixteenth birthday that day with his youth group from White Settlement. He was hit in the back, and the bullet left him paralyzed from the armpits down.

Mary Beth Talley also took a bullet in the back as she tried to protect one of her friends in the back row.

Jaynanne Brown was shot as she was talking with her dear friend, Sydney Browning.

Two other teenagers, Robert DeBord and Nicholas Skinner, were grazed in the shooting.

Hundreds of others suffered the horrible trauma of violence, bloodshed, and death of their loved ones. The psychological effects would continue to arise for years to come.

And the family of Larry Gene Ashbrook would unfairly bear the shame and reproach of their troubled brother.

Any thoughtful consideration would conclude that lives would be irreparably shattered, Wedgwood Church would be destroyed, blame and guilt would be angrily hurled about, and churches would be horribly alienated from one another.

Amazingly, such was not the case.

WHAT HAPPENS NEXT?

When sudden, overwhelming catastrophe occurs in one's life, the first reaction is shock. This is a psychological condition arising in response to traumatic events. It is the emotional aftermath of terror. Because the body cannot maintain the "fight or flight" response, one's emotions go "numb" to protect the nervous system from "shorting out" due to overload.

Symptoms of emotional shock involve a sense of detachment, decreased awareness of one's surroundings, almost as if one is in a dream. During or after a bloody battle, soldiers develop a "thousand-yard stare," an inability to focus on present reality. Sometimes people respond to this acute stress by denial: "This cannot be happening. It must be a dream." This dazed condition can remain for days. If it lasts longer than a month unaddressed, it develops into Post Traumatic Stress Disorder.

Some normal reactions include terror, anger, and outrage, and then depression. Deep questions arise:

- Why did God allow this to happen?
- What could have been done to avoid this?
- Who is to blame?
- Why did I survive?

This last question results in what is called "Survivor's Guilt." "My friends (or loved ones) are dead. Why am I still alive? If anyone deserved to die, it was me!"

In organizations such as churches, schools, or businesses, these issues can result in division and destruction of the organization. Most social structures cannot withstand the trauma of shocking events. Issues of blame and guilt become overwhelming. Whose fault was all this?

The response of leadership brings varied and conflicting reactions. Lawyers counsel silence to avoid prosecutions. The resultant conclusion people often draw is that they are only concerned about self-protection. "No comment" is interpreted as, "We don't care about people's pain."

What is said at funerals can go a long way to heal or to hurt.

What Not to Say

"Well, God must have needed him more than we do."

What does a God who is all-sufficient need with my child/spouse, etc.? This portrays God as arbitrary, at best, and cruel and selfish, at worst. Such conclusions are unfitting for the God of the Bible.

"Don't ask 'Why?' Just keep trusting and believing in God."

Oh really? Jesus was the only man who ever lived without sin of any kind. Yet, in His darkest hour on the cross, He cried out to Heaven, "My God! My God! Why...?" If Jesus can ask "Why," I can too. Telling a brokenhearted victim of violent trauma not to ask "Why?" is like telling a man with a broken leg not to walk with a limp. When we equate honest questioning with sin, we add guilt to their already burdensome load of emotions.

"Think of all the good God will bring out of this."

This is no comfort to grieving friends and loved ones in shock and agony of soul. This is not a scorecard where benefits to others or to the Kingdom can balance out the loss and grief of the empty chair at the Thanksgiving table.

"God must be punishing us for some sin in our lives."

This is one of the worst conclusions, as old as Job's "friends" who sought to add horrible guilt to a wounded, grief-stricken soul. After the terrible tragedy of 9/11, several nationally prominent leaders of the Religious Right opined that it was God's judgment on America for its sins, such as countenancing gay rights. The cause of Christ sometimes suffers more from its defenders than its detractors. In times like this, it is best to try to avoid saying something spiritual or giving advice. The most important thing is the ministry of your presence, your hugs, and your tears. Sometimes, we just need to "weep with those who weep."

Initial Response

One of the first things to do is to arrange funerals—a number of them. Where? When? For Pastors, "What to say?" For family members, how to pay for them? Funerals have become one of the largest expense items for modern families, right after a house and an automobile.

Some in the funeral industry have become experts at playing on people's grief and shock to get them to sign up for overly expensive funeral arrangements. Have someone, a friend or pastor, go with the family to make arrangements. Financial bondage is one of the added burdens in these tragic situations.

Having said that, I have seen at times like these some funeral homes offer drastically reduced prices or even waive them altogether. In a number of situations, incoming gifts or "GoFundMe" accounts have paid for most or all of the expenses.

In our case, so much money came in from around the world that every family's funeral expenses, from casket to lots to markers, and even clothes for the funeral, were paid for by others' generosity. Enough funds were available to pay for counseling for anyone affected, whether they were present at the shooting or not, for years to come.

All hospital bills were funded, including subsequent physical therapy and recovery for those wounded.

A Memorial outside of the church stands with a flagpole and a large granite base containing the pictures and life Scripture verses of each of the victims. It was built with these funds.

My general advice regarding memorials is to resist making quick decisions. One suggestion in our case called for more than $500,000 in construction costs for a memorial that would have dwarfed the church itself!

Decisions, Decisions

Beyond the planning of funerals, our city appropriately wanted a chance to mourn together. In our case, arrangements were made to hold a gathering in Texas Christian University's football stadium. A local pastor and friend, Dr. Michael Dean of Travis Avenue Baptist Church, arranged the details, for which I remain deeply grateful.

Questions such as who to invite (the entire community), who should speak (people from many denominations, including my Catholic brother, the Rev. Dick Beaumont, a local rabbi, and me), and how to avoid our theological differences all had to be addressed.

Our church is blessed to be located in one of the greatest cities in the nation—Fort Worth, Texas. A bond was formed between civic leaders, first responders, fellow churches, and pastors of various denominations. Those relationships have lasted, even to this day. I became the personal prayer partner of the next three police chiefs. Our church began a prayer ministry with the local police division. In short, we realized that not just our church members but also the entire community needed to be involved in the healing process. It brought various factors of the city together. It was a wonderful expression of pastor John Donne's poem: "And therefore never send to know for whom the bell tolls; It tolls for thee."

Other crucial decisions to be made are, "When do we want to meet again?" or "When do we get back to work?" In our situation, it was determined to meet again that Sunday if the police and ATF would allow. In the battle between the Darkness and the Light, we were not going to concede a single inch. We were going to worship our glorious God, even in the midst of our sorrow and the visible evidence of violence in our sanctuary. This is not an easy issue to resolve. Many were terrified about returning to the scene of the carnage, but as I explained it to our staff at a meeting in our living room, "If you fall off a horse, the best thing is to get right back on." We were respectful to those who were just too afraid. One little girl finally agreed with her parents to go back to Sunday school but only if she could wear her tennis shoes in case she had to run again.

On the first Sunday, we asked that only members and friends come as our seating only allowed for 1500. Still, at least 2200 came that Sunday. Some came from as far away as Arizona and Oklahoma. One missionary even flew in from Jordan.

The tension and sense of excitement were surreal. We allowed the TV cameras of one station into the sanctuary as a feeder for the other stations. The world was watching. Do Christians mourn differently?

Two of the victims were choir members, so the choir loft held two empty chairs with their choir robes and long-stemmed roses.

We rose to sing "We Are Standing on Holy Ground" as we took back the territory from the enemy. Then, we declared our tested faith by praising God with the hymn "Great is thy Faithfulness." The atmosphere was electric.

One church from Tulsa, Oklahoma, sent a van full of members who prayer-walked around our property as we worshipped.

And the world looked on as we grieved the loss of our loved ones and lifted our hearts in praise with tearful eyes and broken hearts.

Initial Grieving

How do we process our grief? How do we allow for healthy discussion of broken hearts? If you do not encourage transparent discussion of one's deepest sorrows, if you just "put on a happy face" and stuff your pain, the subconscious grief will return later and paralyze you.

We encouraged our Sunday school leaders to use the time for discussion and group therapy. From young children to senior adults, people shared their grief and pain, fears and questions. In short, we encouraged the body to be the body and to comfort one another with the same comfort they had received from God (2 Corinthians 1:4).

In my Children's Sermon, I reminded them of Humpty Dumpty who "had a great fall." But what all the king's horsemen could not do, God could. He would put the pieces back together again. Then, I preached on Romans 8:28 and reminded the faithful that, although God allows the pain and sorrows of life, He promises to work all things together for our good.

Everyone was encouraged to share. No feelings were deemed illegitimate. No real questions were discouraged. The issue was not so much to find quick answers to those questions but to encourage their expression. We found God could handle our deepest questions and fears.

And, He can handle our anger as well, even when it is directed at Him. One of the most common responses to terrifying events is anger with God. If He is all-powerful—and He is—and if He loves us—and He does—why didn't He do something about this to stop it from happening?

We will deal with these questions in a later chapter. The point here is not to discourage or shame those with these piercing questions. God can handle it. He knows all about our doubts, fears, and questions, so trying to hide them from Him is both futile and foolish. It will lead to deeper emotional consequences.

Feel Your Feelings

On the next Tuesday, our youth met in the evening to talk things out together. Teens tend to listen most to their peers. So, they talked and shared, wept and hugged. Then, we gave them each a marker and permission to do what they had always wanted to do—"tag" the church.

The carpet had all been torn up for replacement, leaving only the concrete floor. They were encouraged to go back into the sanctuary and write down on the cement what they were thinking and feeling, to express their grief and pain at the time of the tragedy. Here are some examples:

- "Dear God, here is where I was when the shooting started. Thank you for protecting me."
- "Thank you, God, for stopping my mom (our Children's Minister) here and keeping her from getting shot. I love her so!"

One of the great blessings our church received was something like 21,000 letters and emails from churches and saints around the world. God's Church was standing with us and praying for us.

What were we to do with all of these? People far more creative than I am decided to wallpaper our halls with them all! We kept them up for three months. As we walked into our church building, you could literally feel the comfort and encouragement of the body of Christ from around the world.

Cards from the Archbishop of Canterbury, from a housewife in Australia, or from a teen from Canada; these expressions of hope and encouragement did much to help in our eventual recovery. I believe that for six months or so, we were the most prayed-for congregation in the world. When I would travel to other churches to speak, they would often ask, "How are you folks doing?"

My standard answer was, "We are doing only because you have been praying. Keep it up!"

One last decision for the initial stages is, "How long should we grieve? How long do we center on our pain and remember the victims?"

There is no stock answer that pleases everyone.

The following Sunday, I began a new series based on our Mission Statement in an effort to find ecclesiastical equilibrium, just to remind us what we are about and not to let the shooting knock us off balance.

The anniversaries of the shooting were times to remember, to mourn healthfully, and to recall God's goodness and faithfulness. It is important to feel your feelings, to express your grief, but not to get locked into morbid, paralyzing sorrow.

But what that looks like, how that expresses itself, is different for each individual church or organization.

Every man's pain is unique.

Soon—all too soon—we become yesterday's news. The camera trucks disappear. The reporters move on to the next story. A New Normal descends.

DEALING WITH THE MEDIA

One of the areas in which organizational leaders have little or no experience or training is the art of dealing with the media in times of crisis. Far too often, we become the victims of every headline hunting journalist, or worse, plagued by wild rumors floating around cyberspace that have little or no basis in facts. As we react to this misinformation, we can easily become defensive and develop an adversarial attitude toward the media.

General Attitudes

One of the problems in this situation is a widespread distrust and disrespect of the press by the general public. According to a 2016 Gallup poll, public confidence in the media has fallen to an all-time low. Only 32 percent of the American public said they have "a great deal" or even "a fair amount" of trust in the mass media. This is an eight percent drop from the previous year. It is the lowest point in Gallup's polling history since they began in 1972.[1] This distrust cuts across political party lines and across generations. At present, only about a third of Americans have any trust at all in the Press.

For the most part, especially during catastrophic events, reporters are viewed as a pack of jackals surrounding a wounded animal. Terms like "fake news" are common. Conservatives despise what they call "the liberal press." Liberals despise what they deem to be propaganda from the right wing. All this is conducive to a situation where one can easily become victimized.

---

[1] https://news.gallup.com/poll/195542/americans-trust-mass-media-sinks-new-low.aspx

Our Experience

On the day after the shooting, NBC's "Today Show" asked for an interview in our home. I was tired, exhausted, and without sleep, but I felt it was a chance to share our spiritual convictions at a time when the world might be listening.

A news team consisting of a reporter, a sound man, and a camera man set things up in our living room. I was given an earpiece, and we were plugged in live to Katie Couric and the Today Show in New York City. As they were about to cut away to a commercial break to be followed by our interview, one of the studio crew decided to read an email in response to their coverage. It went something like this:

"Congratulations, all you media people! I hope you can sleep tonight knowing you make your living on other people's 'tragedies.'"

I remember thinking, "That is not fair at all. That is a classic case of 'shooting the messenger.' Reporters are only trying to do their job just like the rest of us. And where would our nation be without the constitutionally protected blessing of a free press?"

Where, indeed!

After the interview, the media team expressed their sincere gratitude to me for allowing them the opportunity to come into our home and answer questions directly. In fact, every journalist I talked with in those dark days was respectful, gentle, and grateful. And they always ended by saying, "If there is anything we can do to help in any way, let us know."

So, I decided to call them on it.

"Well, there is something you can do," I said.

"What is it? Tell us."

"Would you allow me the privilege of praying for you before you leave?"

"Of course! Please do," they responded surprisingly.

This is how I prayed for them and for every crew we spoke with:

"Dear Sovereign Father, thank You for giving us hope in our time of darkness and an anchor in our storm. I pray for these reporters who have to witness shocking things every day. Protect them from developing scars upon their hearts or becoming jaded. Protect their families while they are away from home. Help them to get the story out and to get the story straight. Do not let their editors skew the story into sound bites that misinterpret the truth.

"And, dear Jesus, may they come to know You as the only hope when the darkness descends and their own lives fall apart. In Your precious Name I pray, Amen."

When I looked up from praying, all three were wiping tears away, and they thanked me profusely. It was the first time they had ever been prayed for in their job. And, they were grateful.

Media as Mission Field

I began to see reporters and journalists as a mission field. They really are just ordinary people with the same joys and heartaches, problems and needs, trials and triumphs as all of us.

So, I determined I would ask to pray for them after every encounter. No one has ever refused. No one has ever even expressed resentment. Many have wiped away tears.

In fact, in subsequent years, on anniversaries or after other shocking events, some of the same journalists have come back and told me, "I always look forward to being prayed over."

Our church has found great favor, as a result, from the media. I have never seen one iota of harmful criticism or a bad report. We have been blessed indeed!

I believe it is, in part at least, due to our dealing with the media with respect and concern for them.

"Do Unto Others"

Frankly, most of our problems with the media and with others could be greatly improved if we just followed Jesus a little more closely and practiced the Golden Rule. If we could see them as people like us with jobs to do, deadlines to meet, editors to satisfy, and families to support, perhaps we could cut each other a little slack and treat them as we would like to be treated.

There are a few principles that I have found beneficial in dealing with the Public in general and reporters in particular in times of crisis:

Number One: Tell the truth! Numbers 32:23 says, "...and be sure your sin will find you out." We have seen it repeatedly in recent years that the attempt to cover up always brings more scorn, shame, and regret than simply admitting the worst crimes and mistakes. If you cannot come out with statements openly for legal or other reasons, say as much as you can say, and say it humbly and graciously.

Number Two: Be as transparent and open as you can be. If we are forthcoming and proactive, we can gain a measure of control of the issue and become less vilified by rumors.

Number Three: Be compassionate. Be sure to portray a heartfelt concern for the victims in the catastrophe. The victims and their families need to know of our compassion for their loss. Studies have been shown that doctors involved in malpractice incidents are far less likely to be sued if they just show up and express their humble regret for the circumstances, regardless of culpability. Just let them know you care!

Number Four: Be respectful and polite. We are living in an age of incivility when people under pressure lose their cool at the drop of a hat. Domestic violence and road rage have become all too common. We cannot excuse thoughtless rants by explaining that we were under pressure. My father always said, "What's down in the well will come up in the bucket." In other words, you are what you are under pressure. If you squeeze an orange, you don't get Coca-Cola. There is no excuse for disrespect and impoliteness.

Free Publicity!

Wedgwood is a church tucked away in a residential community off the beaten path. It was built in 1960 when the going theory of church growth was that, since the school is the center of society, a church should go find a new school with a vacant lot across the street and build a church building there.

We used to congratulate our visitors for finding us on a Sunday morning. We would tell them, "You are either here because you want to be, or you are lost because we are not on the way to anything." We never had any money for advertising. If we did, we might have billed ourselves as "The Church That's Worth the Search!"

Now the whole world was camped on our doorsteps wanting to get our opinions and reactions! It was time to step up to the plate and deliver. How often do Katie Couric, Larry King, Vice President Al Gore, President Bill Clinton, and the major networks come calling, asking how you are doing and what you have to say?

The fact that this was our most tragic hour made our testimony all the more compelling. Either Christ makes a difference, or He does not. Either Christians live and die differently, or we have been blowing smoke for 2,000 years!

The clock was ticking; the spotlight was on. It was time to stand and deliver.

As a result of all this exposure and because we found favor with the press, Wedgwood became a "destination church" for the next several years. Instead of our having to scour the city for prospects, people would come to Fort Worth looking for us. This was one of the reasons why God gave us dynamic growth for the next five years.

The interest of the media was our opportunity to get the Message out. As someone has well said, "Never waste a crisis."

MAN'S DEEPEST QUESTION: THE PROBLEM OF EVIL

I t is the oldest and deepest question encountered in human experience. From Job of ancient days to the martyrs crying from beneath the throne of God Himself, the cry rings out: "Why do the righteous suffer? Why does evil abound?"

Philosophers call it "The Problem of Evil." Theologians refer to it as "Theodicy." The question put simply is this: "If God is all-powerful, which He must be by definition, and if God loves us, then why do the innocent suffer so? Why do children and youth, men and women die violently for no apparent reason? Why do storms carry away the just and the unjust alike?"

A Universal Problem

This question is not exclusive to Christianity. Every great religion is driven to attempt to find an answer. The conclusion for Muslims is Fate, or "Kismet," which means that Allah has predetermined everything, that every event in our lives has been "written" in Allah's Book. But this seems to shatter the sense of human freedom and responsibility that is inherent within us all.

Buddhism finds no solution to the question but teaches that one must achieve the frame of mind in which one simply does not care. Indifference to pain and suffering, which are universal, is the only way to rise above the evil that surrounds us.

Hinduism says little on the subject except to recognize the ever presence of human suffering and to try to pacify the more than 300 million gods by keeping religious rituals and hoping your Karma allows for better conditions in the next reincarnation.

Modern philosophers from Marxism to Skinnerian Behaviorism tend to degenerate into strict determinism that gives up any idea of human freedom, as B.F. Skinner's *Beyond Freedom and Human Dignity* explains.

Existentialism, the most prevalent anti-philosophy of our day, merely gives up all hope of finding meaningful answers to life's deepest questions and concludes that life is absurd and meaningless.

But that doesn't stop us from asking "Why?" when tragedy strikes. The demand for justice, as Immanuel Kant observed, is universal. Like little children complain, "Mommy, it's not fair!" we cry out to the heavens, "Why do bad things happen to good people?"

Christian Extremes

Even among Christians who share a common faith in Christ and the authority of the Bible, there are myriads of conflicting conclusions.

One of these would be what is known as Hyper-Calvinism. These are the followers of John Calvin, St. Augustine, and perhaps the apostle Paul who, because they emphasize the sovereignty of an all-powerful God, tend to downplay human freedom and accountability. They hold that God has foreordained every event in our lives in particular and in history in general. But, to many, this seems to make human beings, who are made in the image of God, mere robots or puppets.

In response to this extreme position, there are people known as Arminians, named after the Dutch theologian Jacobus Arminius, who disagreed with Calvin and insisted that people are free to choose or reject God. They say that

God's grace is not irresistible and His purposes are dependent on man's response.

In recent years, this position has led to "Open Theism," which holds that there are some things God must not know about, since to foreknow events would be to predetermine them, thus canceling out human freedom. In so doing, they cancel out not only God's omnipotence but His omniscience as well. This conclusion is patently unacceptable.

Far more popular is the rather recent development of what some call the "Prosperity Gospel." This is the conviction that God's purposes for His children are health, wealth, and happiness. Sickness, disease, and tragedy are the direct consequences of sin and unbelief. If one's faith is strong and sin is subdued, the results will be material prosperity and physical health. Like Job's erstwhile friends, one must simply confess one's sins to God, and then one's favorable circumstances will be restored again. Unfortunately, this approach tends to add guilt to one's sorrow and pain.

The Bible on Suffering

The Bible has much to say about pain, suffering, afflictions, and tribulations. Nowhere does it indicate that God's people are immune to problems or difficulties.

One of Jesus' not-so-precious promises is, "In the world you will have tribulation" (John 16:33).

One of Job's so-called friends spoke truth when he observed, "For man is born for trouble, As sparks fly upward" (Job 5:7).

The apostle Peter wrote to believers scattered throughout the Roman Empire and warned them, "Beloved, do not be surprised at the fiery ordeal among you...as though some strange thing were happening to you" (1 Peter 4:12).

To the church at Philippi he explained, "For to you it has been granted (graciously given)...to suffer for His sake" (Philippians 1:29).

King David of the Old Testament testifies, "Many are the afflictions of the righteous, But the Lord delivers him out of (not from) them all" (Psalm 34:19).

These are only a few of many, many passages that tell us that trials, afflictions, and suffering should not only be expected, but also even embraced. I will speak more about that later.

Americans have sought to create a pain-free society. Painkillers engender billions of dollars in sales as most of us "haven't got time for the pain," as the sales jingle goes. But a pain-free existence does not bring us Nirvana, as Aldus Huxley explains in his dystopian novel, *Brave New World*. Instead, it produces a grey society where creativity is stifled and mediocrity abounds. There, people are not grateful, as they have no difficulties with which to compare their pain-free existence. Phil Yancey eloquently reminds us that a pain-free existence is realized in the dread illness known as Hanson's Disease or leprosy! The nerve endings are dead, and the results are catastrophic. Pain is a necessary component to health.

Theology and Pain

In developing one's theology, it is critical to determine one's starting point.

One University of Missouri Philosophy professor supposedly had a final exam with only one question: "How do you get to the St. Louis Arch?" Almost all of the students had been there and wrote detailed accounts of the proper interstate roads and exits to take once one got to St. Louis. But the only student who passed the exam wrote two words: "From where?"

Your starting point is crucial in plotting your destination.

If you begin to formulate a theology from man's point of view, your ultimate conclusions will be deeply influenced thereby. Most modern worldviews tend to make much of man and, consequently, little of God. To them, man's importance is central; God's is peripheral. Man's viewpoints and powers are emphasized to the diminishment of God's.

Once the issue of epistemology (How do I know what I know?) is settled, and I am assuming the authority of Scripture here, then the initial question is, "What is God like?" All other answers are derived from that primary premise.

There are many cogent and pertinent things we could say about the nature and attributes of God. Certainly, His holiness, justice, mercy, and grace are all essential to the character of the God of the Bible. But the most germane consideration in the context of any discussion about the Problem of Evil has to do with the sovereignty of God. Questioning God's sovereignty is to ask, "Is God in charge of the universe He created? Are there places in the cosmos that are beyond His control or times when He bows out of the picture?" This is the conclusion Rabbi Harold Kushner makes in his popular book, *When Bad Things Happen to Good People*. The book arises out of the author's personal crisis when his 11-year-old son died of progeria, a tragic disease that causes a child to age at an alarming rate until he dies of the onset of old age and its complications.

Faced with the seeming paradox of a loving God who is also in sovereign control of the universe and the horrendous evils that abound in the human condition, Kushner was struck with an impossible dilemma. Apparently, the author felt forced to choose between the two and chose to side with the loving, benevolent God. Therefore, there must be instances where circumstances are beyond God's control, as in the case of Kushner's son.

This conclusion, however, is logically and scripturally untenable. He, by definition, is God Almighty, for whom nothing is impossible (Genesis 18:14; Matthew 19:26), except that which would be contrary to His nature (that is to lie, to sin, to die).

Moreover, the scriptures are replete with references to God's love, mercy, and goodness. God is Love personified.

Anything less than a sovereign, majestic God whose love and mercy endure forever leaves us with a Being who is unworthy of our love, devotion, and worship.

The Responsibility of Man

Having established the clear teaching of Scripture regarding the sovereignty of God, the question that now begs our attention is this: If God is actively in control of every molecule in the universe, as the Dutch theologian Abraham Kuyper contends, how can we maintain that human beings are free moral agents? How can God hold us accountable for our actions when He has predetermined them all? Does this teaching not make robots of us all?

Let it be here stated that the Bible clearly teaches repeatedly that we are free moral agents and we are responsible for the consequences of those choices and actions:

- "...and be sure your sin will find you out." (Numbers 32:23)
- "For we must all appear before the judgment seat of Christ, so that each one may be recompensed for his deeds...." (2 Corinthians 5:10)

In the Garden of Eden, Adam and Eve were told to enjoy it all with one clear exception: the Forbidden Fruit. The consequences of that fatal choice are tragically with us still.

Every command in the Bible is testimony to God's call for us to choose righteousness and eschew evil. Consequences for refusal are inescapable. Cain is banished for his murder of his brother. Sodom and Gomorrah are destroyed for their evil practices. Even God's own chosen people are disciplined for their disobedience and exiled for their rebellion.

So, how does one reconcile these two seemingly oppositional teachings?

In a word, I cannot.

But, in Charles Spurgeon's words, "Why should I try to reconcile two friends? These two facts are parallel lines; I cannot make them unite, but you cannot make them cross each other."

Limits to Human Freedom

Let it be said here that there are limits to human "free will." First, there are natural, physical limits. We are finite, mortal beings. We cannot act outside or beyond our human, physical limits. I am a 71-year-old, five-foot-ten, somewhat overweight man. No matter how much I desire it, I will never be able to dunk a basketball or play in the NBA or fly under my own power.

Secondly, my fallen, sinful nature will not allow me to live a holy, sinless life this side of Heaven. My natural propensity towards selfishness and sin brings a constant struggle. "Prone to wander, Lord, I feel it; Prone to leave the God I love." In this case, I am not alone.

Randy Alcorn, in his insightful book, *Hand in Hand: The Beauty of God's Sovereignty and Meaningful Human Choice*, gives several illustrations that help clarify the issue.

Alcorn asks his readers to imagine a ship on the ocean. God is the owner, the captain of the ship, and mankind are the passengers. The passengers are free to move about, converse, be kind or not to each other, and generally, order their lives as they wish. The captain, however, keeps an overall semblance of order on the ship and determines the course and destination of the ship and its passengers.

The obvious implication is that, in some sense, humans are free to make choices as their conscience, reason, or selfish desires direct them. There are natural consequences for each choice. A sovereign God, however, orchestrates every human decision, good or bad, to ultimately result in the praise of His glory.

Like all illustrations, there are limitations with this one. While it may shed a measure of light on the problem, we are still left with questions unanswered. What possible good could come from the violent death of innocent babies? While some suffering may eventually result in an ultimate benefit, does that necessarily make up for the agony and pain experienced by many? Does the eventual establishment of the State of Israel make up for the horrific life and death of millions of Jews in the Holocaust? Is God some kind of Cosmic Accountant playing computer games with human misery?

I first began to contemplate the depths of this issue as a freshman in college. In my "Introduction to Christian Faith" class, I first learned of the mysterious doctrine of election and predestination. My mind was blown away as I pondered the implications. I wrestled with that for years.

I am still wrestling.

As I riddled my professor with questions, he eventually told me that my questions were well taken and profitable, but that while I might not be able to solve all the riddles of the paradox, by God's grace I might be able to come to the place where I could live with the unanswered questions.

That prediction has proven true. I have come to treasure those mysterious doctrines.

I have noticed, however, that when life falls apart, all of us tend to become at least partial Calvinists. In ways we do not understand, for reasons we cannot fathom, we all insist that, somehow, God is in control, knows what He is doing, and loves us all the while.

What is the alternative? God does not exist? Unthinkable! Things are out of God's control? Preposterous! There is no purpose or plan, just a chance happening? Absurd!

At some point, we must realize that we are left with a measure of mystery. But, does this particular mystery not come at precisely the place where we might expect it to appear? At the very spot where the sovereign activity of an infinite God comes in contact with the free choices and actions of finite man? In fact, if we could explain this perfectly, wouldn't it be reason enough to reject that worldview? Deuteronomy 29:29 tells us, "The secret things belong to the Lord our God, but those things which are revealed belong to us and to our children."

When my children were little, my wife and I tried to raise them to become increasingly independent and responsible. So, we granted them a measure of freedom to make some decisions on their own. As they grew and matured, we expanded the boundaries of their freedom.

But, whenever their free choices conflicted with their parents' plans, guess whose freedom won out? At times, they complained about our restrictions, but every one was for their good and out of a heart of love.

Sadly, we were not always right in our parenting.

Happily, Father God never makes mistakes

WHY?

Dr. James Dobson, in his book, *When God Doesn't Make Sense*, tells the story of a man condemned to life in prison under solitary confinement in a pitch-black cell. The only thing to occupy his mind was a marble, which he repeatedly threw against the wall, listened as it bounced and rolled across the cold stone floor, and then recovered after groping in the darkness, only to repeat the exercise again and again. This seemingly futile exercise seemed to keep him from going mad in the darkness of that cell.

Then one day, he threw his marble up in the air and heard nothing, only the silence reverberating in the darkness of his cell. Heartbroken and desperate at the disappearance of his toy, deeply disturbed by his inability to explain it, the man grieved, pondered, and agonized. He eventually went insane and died.

When the guards came to remove his body, they noticed a strange thing. In a corner, a spider had woven a huge web, and there was a marble caught in its strands.

"Strange," said one of the guards. "I wonder how that got there?"

How, indeed.

It seems to be woven into the DNA of humanity to question "Why?" concerning the inexplicable mysteries of life. We rail against the seeming cosmic injustices of life. We debate about the causes and effects of our triumphs and defeats. We long to discover not only the "how" of the human condition but the "whys."

It is often a futile endeavor. In the cartoon series *The Simpsons*, Homer has somehow gotten the Almighty to agree to answer his sincere question regarding the purpose of life. But, as God begins to explain things, the time is up for the show, the credits begin to roll, and they break for a commercial. Homer is left with no purpose to his life, no answers to his questions.

But we cannot help ourselves. Our first response when tragedy strikes is to lift our eyes to Heaven and, from the depths of our soul, cry, "Why, oh Lord?"

Is it a Sin to Ask "Why?"

Some well-intentioned, seemingly spiritual folks will chastise brokenhearted people for asking the why question, claiming that it is somehow sinful, exhibiting a lack of faith. On the contrary, sometimes asking God for an explanation is the greatest act of faith we can engender given the circumstances. That they still believe enough in God to question Him after they are left with nothing but the shattered pieces of their hopes and dreams shows evidence of a deep and abiding faith.

As noted earlier, if God's perfect and holy Son could cry out to His Father from the cross, "My God, My God, why...?" certainly, it is not a sin for us to do the same.

The Purpose of Pain

Western culture in general has little or no understanding of the positive effects of suffering. Other than momentary sweat and toil in the gym ("No pain, no gain"), pain is disdained and to be avoided at all costs.

Not so in Scripture.

One of the biblical purposes of suffering is that God uses adversity to train His followers in obedience to His will. David records in Psalm 119:67, "Before I was afflicted I went astray, But now I keep Your word." Just as a child must be disciplined in order to grow in obedience, so God uses adversity to train His saints to walk in the way of righteousness.

Along the same vein, God uses trials and disappointments to develop strong Christian character. As the writer James tells us in James 1:2-3, we should "count it all joy, my brothers, when you encounter various trials, knowing that the testing of your faith produces endurance."

The large and influential Willow Creek Church near Chicago once conducted an in-depth survey of thousands of its members as to the primary factors involved in their spiritual growth. The single, most influential thing was not powerful preaching, not inspired worship nor dynamic small groups, though these all had their place in the process. The one thing that was most effective in their spiritual maturation process was pain, trials, hardships, and suffering! As their faith was tested, it grew stronger. There are lessons in life that can only be learned in the Valley of Pain and Disappointment.

Another purpose for suffering and pain is that we might be able to bring comfort and encouragement to others who are in the midst of afflictions. Second Corinthians 1:3-4 reminds us of the "God of all comfort, who comforts us in all our affliction so that we will be able to comfort those who are in any affliction with the comfort with which we ourselves are comforted by God."

After the shooting in 1999, God gave Wedgwood a wonderful ministry of healing and comfort. People with broken hearts were drawn to us. I was able to speak to nearly 100 different audiences in the 12 months following the shooting without missing a single Sunday in the pulpit at Wedgwood. Our counseling and caring ministry grew. In a very real way, I was able to process my own grief by telling the story of our sorrow repeatedly and letting God heal me by using me to bring comfort and healing to others.

There is another, more difficult to understand, purpose for suffering. That is to draw us into closer intimacy with God. There is no shortcut to being drawn into intimacy with Christ without sharing in the fellowship of His suffering.

The Apostle Paul's deepest desire was to "know Him and the power of His resurrection and the fellowship of His sufferings..." (Philippians 3:10). When we suffer deeply, only then can we begin to understand what He endured so we might be reconciled to God.

One other purpose behind our suffering, though this list is by no means exhaustive, is so that we might bring glory to God. No single thing brings more glory to God and distress to the enemy than when God's saints choose to praise Him in the midst of the storm, even when there are no answers.

Job lost virtually everything he had: house, lands, crops, animals, family, health, and reputation. His wife enjoined him to "curse God and die." His friends told him to confess his sins, for which he was suffering such pain. He plunged into suicidal depression; he angrily voiced his complaints to God. Yet, in the midst of the darkness, he cried, "Though He slay me, yet will I trust Him" (Job 13:15). Lucifer's prediction was thwarted by Job's faithfulness, even in the darkness.

It is interesting to note that throughout the book of Job, God never provides an answer to why Job is suffering so. When God finally shows up near the end, He does not give a detailed explanation of the Problem of Evil. Instead, He delivers the longest speech by God recorded in the Bible. He takes Job on a grand tour of the universe, pointing out all the greatness of the expanse of the cosmos, and asks Job if he was there when God established the stars of the heavens and created the creatures of the sea. Job finally gets a glimpse of the greatness and majesty of Almighty God and covers his mouth in humility.

But God does not stop there. He begins Round Two and shows Job the wonders of creation even further and asks him whether he can match God's creative and sustaining power. Job finally responds in repentance in dust and ashes.

It appears that God's answer to the question of theodicy is not "Why?" but "Who?" More important than processing the solution to the Problem of Evil is that we know the God who is sovereign over all things and that we humble ourselves before Him whose Name is Jehovah-Shamma, the God who is there!

When we do not know the answers to life's deepest problems, it is enough to know God and to be assured that nothing can ever separate us from His love.

Margery Kempe (1373-1438) was married to a local official in her town in England. She bore him 14 children, and after he died, she suffered a total emotional breakdown. Plagued with doubts and fears, she sought God for answers. Her search for peace led her on a pilgrimage to the Holy Land and Rome. In the process, Margery received many dreams and visions and became the spiritual advisor to numerous theologians, noblemen, and church leaders.

Her life was transformed when she was touched by the grace of God and the power of His love.

When one personally knows the great "Who" of the Universe and that nothing can separate us from His love (Romans 8:38-39), one can endure any "How?" or "Why?" life might throw their way.

Lies Christians Believe

Establishing an attitude and environment for healing and recovery from grief and trauma involves not only the construction of a biblical view of suffering but also the identification of the lies and falsehoods that are commonly held.

One of the most common myths held by Christians today is the belief that *"God will never give you more than you can handle."* I have seen this on kitchen walls and cards meant for encouragement. The truth is that God is in the breaking business! As long as we can handle our circumstances, we do not really need God. God only truly enters our lives when we are desperate for Him.

Another common myth is that "*God wants us to be happy*." This is usually used as an excuse for some activity we know is wrong or unscriptural, such as divorcing our spouse. While it is true that in God's presence there is "fullness of joy" (Psalm 16:11), God is primarily concerned not so much about our happiness as our holiness. Happiness is never discovered by flaunting God's precepts.

Almost universal in its appeal is the half-truth that "*God is Love*." This truth becomes a lie when it is seen as all-inclusive and all-encompassing. Modern man often interprets this as divine indulgence: that no matter what I do or how I act, God, like a celestial Grandfather, merely pats us on the head and assures us that we are okay. But, God's Word tells us that none of us is okay: "There is none righteous, no, not one" (Romans 3:10-12). It is only when we realize this that we are driven to cast ourselves on the mercy of God. God's love does not trump His holiness.

Another debilitating lie that arises in times of trial is expressed in the words of an old Gospel song, "*Nobody Knows the Trouble I've Seen*." The implication is that I am the only one to experience the pain and sorrow I am going through. First Corinthians 10:13 tells us, "No temptation has overtaken you but such as is common to man." In other words, my heartache is not the first time dreams have been dashed or lives broken. There is healing and comfort in realizing I am not alone in my grief or despair.

Finally, one of the common misunderstandings following traumatic grief is the idea that "*I will never be happy again*," or "*My sorrow will never end*." One of my favorite phrases in Scripture is "and it came to pass." It—grief, sorrow, and pain—did not come to stay. There are seasons of grief, and even depression, but "joy comes in the morning" (Psalm 30:5). As Jesus explained to the disciples in the upper room, "Now is your time of grief, but I will see you again and you will rejoice, and no one will take away your joy" (John 16:22).

Life's Ultimate Purpose

Your reason for living will determine your response to life's trials. If you think life's ultimate purpose is for God to provide for you a carefree and happy life, then pain and sorrow will prove to be intolerable. Someone has said that attitude is everything. Most of us are only six inches from success. Those are the six inches between our ears!

Scripture teaches that God's ultimate purpose for our lives is to "glorify God, and to enjoy him forever," according to the Westminster Shorter Catechism. Romans 8:28-29 says that God "works all things together for the good of those who love Him," not just to make us happy and comfortable, but that we might become "conformed to the image of His Son." When one aspires to that, then afflictions and pain are seen as necessary conditions to the eventual outcome of becoming Christ-like.

As Larry Crabb explains in his study of the book of Ruth, *The Meaning of Shattered Dreams*, most of us are dreaming the wrong dreams. Like Naomi, we dream of loving spouses, family, and friends in familiar and comfortable surroundings. However, God uprooted her from her hometown and took her to a land of strangers where she was the alien. Then, her husband died, followed by her two sons, leaving her without any grandchildren to carry on the family legacy.

"Don't call me Naomi (Pleasant)," she lamented to her daughter-in-law, Ruth. "Call me Mara (Bitter); for the Almighty has dealt very bitterly with me" (Ruth 1:20).

But God has shattered Naomi's dreams, and ours, to make us desperate for Him, not just His blessings.

When my children were very young, I would sometimes take off from work and take them to a nearby park. They would run through the woods after a butterfly or new adventures, leaving their dad behind. So, I would hide behind a tree and wait. Finally, "Daddy!" would pierce the air, and I would step out and reveal myself to them once again. The point was that I wanted them to enjoy me at least as much as the delights of the park.

So, God, at times, hides Himself (Isaiah 45:15) so that we might long for His Presence as well as the blessings He brings.

Your reason for living will determine your response to life's trials.

THE ISSUE OF FORGIVENESS

Several weeks after the shooting, a journalist from the denominational newspaper of the church in which Larry Gene Ashbrook had been raised visited me in my office. After expressing his condolences and discussing subsequent events, he stated, "Of course, it is way too soon to even consider forgiveness."

He was wrong. It is never too soon to begin the process of forgiveness.

The Bible on Forgiveness

Serious Christ-followers have no choice regarding the issue of forgiveness. One of Jesus' final words from the cross was, "Father, forgive them" (Luke 23:34). One of the key components of the Lord's Prayer is, "And forgive us our debts, As we forgive our debtors" (Matthew 6:12).

As it is essential to the very nature of God to forgive sins, so too, it is an essential characteristic of His people to forgive others. When Jesus declared that the one who is unwilling to forgive and show mercy to those in his debt would be turned over to the torturers (Matthew 18:21-35), it was not to say that we can earn forgiveness by forgiving others, but rather, when one truly discovers how indebted we are to Christ for forgiving us, we cannot help but forgive others. An unforgiving heart is one that has not experienced God's boundless mercy.

As I shared with the journalist, no matter how badly I am treated, I did far worse to Jesus, and He forgave me. The age-old question of who killed Christ is answered simply, "I did." It was for *my* sins Christ suffered and died. It was for *my* iniquities He was cut off from the Father. It was *my* transgressions that forced Christ to bear the curse. The more aware I become of my responsibility for the death of the Prince of Heaven, the more petty and trite my silly grudges appear.

It is this divine attribute of forgiveness that sets Christianity apart from other world religions. Nearly all religions encourage us to love our neighbor and hate our enemies. But Jesus commands us to "love your enemies" (Matthew 5:44) and "turn your other cheek" (Matthew 5:39).

When lapsed Muslim author, Salman Rushdie, wrote his disrespectful book, *The Satanic Verses*, in 1989, the Ayatollah Khomeini declared, "Even if Salman Rushdie repents and becomes the most pious man of all time, it is incumbent on every Muslim to employ everything he's got, his life and wealth, to send him to hell."[2]

The Mongolian Tatar king, Genghis Khan, was supposedly asked, "What is the best thing in life?" In spite of the fact that he regularly treated his conquered foes graciously, once the fighting was over, he responded, "To crush your enemies, to see them fall at your feet—to take their horses and goods and hear the lamentation of their women."[3]

German poet Heinrich Heine wrote, "We should forgive our enemies, but only after they are hanged first."

Even President John F. Kennedy said, "Forgive your enemies, but never forget their names."

The Effects of Unforgiveness

Recent scientific studies have discovered that the dorsal stratum in the human brain is the part that processes the pleasure of anticipated rewards. It

---

[2] https://www.nytimes.com/1989/02/20/world/khomeini-spurns-rushdie-regrets-and-reiterates-threat-of-death.html
[3] Harold Lamb, *Genghis Khan: The Emperor of All Men* (International Collectors Library: 1927), 106-107.

has shown to positively light up with stimulation at the prospect of revenge. "Revenge is sweet," we all agree. Evidently, it is also highly stimulating to the brain.

It is also deadly. Toxic.

Witness the centuries-old strife in Northern Ireland, the racial cleansing in the Balkans, the battles between the Sunnis and the Shiites in the Middle East, the Hutus versus the Tutsis in Rwanda, and the Hatfields and McCoys in Appalachia.

The fatal flaw in the Law of Revenge is that it never settles the score. One is always required to strike back. It is like living life in the bumper car arcade. As we are bumped, we bump back, like siblings playing "Got you back!" The problem is never resolved, only escalated.

Mahatma Gandhi has been attributed with saying, "An eye for an eye leaves the whole world blind."

Refusal to forgive is the insistence of drinking the poison one intended for his worst enemy. You start by holding a grudge; you end with the grudge holding you.

Forgiveness Is Not...

There are many widely-held beliefs regarding forgiveness that are patently untrue. Robert English, in the book, *To Live and Forget*, lists some of these:

Forgiveness is **NOT**:
1. FORGETTING: Deep hurts can rarely be wiped out of one's awareness.
2. RECONCILIATION: Reconciliation involves two people. Many are unaware or unwilling to enter the process and repair the relationship.

3. CONDONING: Forgiveness does not excuse the egregiousness of the hurtful deeds or words. Condoning evil is nearly as wrong as committing it.

4. DISMISSING: Forgiveness involves taking the offense seriously, not passing it off as inconsequential or insignificant.

5. PARDONING: A pardon is a legal transaction that releases an offender from the consequences or penalty of his offense. Forgiveness is a personal transaction that releases the one offended from the offender. Sin brings consequences that must be met.

The Process of Forgiveness

It is important to note that forgiveness is not a feeling but a choice. Sometimes, we beat ourselves up because of what we are feeling. It is not sinful or wrong to feel emotions. Emotions just are; as such, they are difficult to control or manage. Even Jesus found His emotions to be out of control as He sweat great drops of blood in the garden of Gethsemane prior to His crucifixion.

The error comes when we allow our emotions to dictate our actions.

Lewis Smedes explains the emotional stages of forgiveness:

- First, you HURT. Your heart is broken, pained, wounded.
- Then, you HATE. This is a natural reaction to emotional pain. One harbors deep resentment towards the one who caused the pain.
- Finally, you HEAL. Over the process of time, you choose to view the perpetrator as God does, as one whom God loves and for whom Christ died. You seek to understand him and why he acted the way he did.

The choices in the healing process are manifold. To begin with, one must refuse revenge. Allow God the responsibility of balancing the scales of justice in His own time and way.

The second choice is to perceive the offender as a person—to try to understand him and the reasons for his injurious words or actions.

Thirdly, one must choose to hope for their happiness, even invest in their well-being. As a young pastor, I was called to the local hospital to meet with a man from a neighboring county who was suffering from heart disease, high blood pressure, and pre-stroke conditions, including chest pains and sleeplessness. His very life was in peril.

He shared with me that his brother was profligately spending their parents' inheritance with no regard for his wishes and concerns. The patient was eaten up with bitterness and anger.

"I am a Christian," he explained, "and I know I should forgive him. But, I just cannot get over my fury towards him, and it is killing me!"

I was led to counsel him to return home and offer his brother all of the inheritance, to invest in his well-being. What price did he put on his own physical and emotional health?

I explained that Christ taught in the Sermon on the Mount, "For where your treasure is, there will your heart be also" (Matthew 6:21). In other words, what you invest in will naturally bring with it feelings of hope for success and peace.

Six months later, I received a phone call from the patient saying the chest pains were gone and he was sleeping well. He was grateful for the wonderful grace of forgiveness.

Examples

Historian Michael Hart has written a book called *The One Hundred* in which he catalogs history's top 100 most influential people. In it, he places Jesus Christ in third place. While he admits to Jesus' obvious unmatched superiority as a religious leader and ethical teacher, his main objection is the failure of Christ's followers to practice His precepts.

While Hart's observations are generally accurate, there have been exceptions to this failure. Early Christians tended to be far more faithful to the teachings of Christ than present-day disciples. For the first several centuries, Christians were almost universally pacifists, praying for their persecutors, even while they died. It was this countercultural lifestyle that caused them to "turn the world upside down."

In time, as Christians became more organized and acculturated, they lost their distinctiveness. Instead of loving their enemies, they declared crusades against them, squabbling with and denouncing one another with even more vitriol.

Deep divisions, Holy wars, and Inquisitions were called in the name of God.

There have, however, been notable exceptions.

Towards the end of the 20th Century, the evil system of Apartheid in South Africa was torn down as people of color were given equal status. Everyone expected a blood bath of vengeance after decades of cruel oppression. But it did not happen.

Nelson Mandela taught the world a lesson in grace when he emerged, after 27 years in prison, to become the new President. Astonishingly, he invited his jailer to sit with him on the inauguration platform!

Mandela placed Bishop Desmond Tutu in charge of the Truth and Reconciliation Commission to reverse the pattern of revenge. The new rules were this: if a white official would voluntarily face his accusers, confess his crime, and acknowledge his guilt, all charges would be dropped.

One particular instance involved a policeman named Van de Brock. He shamefully confessed that he and others had shot and killed an 18-year-old boy and then burned the body, turning it in the fire like a piece of meat in order to destroy the evidence. Eight years later, he returned to the same house and seized the boy's father. The wife was forced to watch as the policeman bound her husband on a woodpile, poured gasoline over it, and ignited it.

Philip Yancey describes the electrified courtroom. There was silence there as the elderly woman, who had lost both her husband and son so cruelly, responded to the confession. She said she wanted Van de Brock to go with her to the place where they had burned her loved ones and gather the dust so they could give her loved ones a proper burial. With downcast eyes, the officer agreed.

Then, she added, "Mr. Van de Brock took all my family away from me, and I still have a lot of love to give. Twice a month, I would like for him to come to the ghetto and spend a day with me so I can be a mother to him. And I would like Mr. Van de Brock to know that he is forgiven by God, and that I forgive him too. I would like to embrace him so he can know my forgiveness is real."[4]

Spontaneously, the courtroom broke out singing "Amazing Grace." But Van de Brock never heard the music. He had fainted, overwhelmed by love and forgiveness that only God can give.

The Graffiti on the Floor

On the Tuesday evening after the shooting, some 300 of our youth and parents met together at the church to try to talk things out. The funerals were done, but the long process of healing was just beginning.

After several hours of tears, discussion, and prayer, our leaders gave the youth markers and permission to "tag" the church. The blood-soaked carpet had been torn up for replacement, leaving only the cold concrete floor. They were encouraged to express their thoughts and emotions on the floor.

---

[4] Philip Yancey, *Grace Notes: Daily Readings with a Fellow Pilgrim* (Zondervan: 2009).

Back at the spot where the shooter took his life, a 16-year-old girl left this message: "Dear Larry Ashbrook, I do not know why you came into my church and killed my friends, but because of Calvary, I forgive you."

Beneath this incredible message was a picture of a hill with three crosses.

The Ashbrook Family

Sometime during the weekend of the shooting, amidst the funerals and memorial services, the thought crossed my mind, "What about the Ashbrook family? Is anyone ministering to them?"

I expressed this concern to the leading detective in charge of the investigation and requested that he ask the family if we could meet with them. They had come to Fort Worth to donate their brother's organs to science and to have his body cremated. They were gathered at their lawyer's office downtown when my church Administrator, Mike Holton, and I met with them.

We expressed our concern for them and our conviction that none of them were in any way at fault. They had already received hate mail and anonymous threats. Then, we prayed together.

It was not a long meeting, but it was an important one. Six months later, we received a call from a nearby church of the Ashbrook's denomination. The family had sold their brother's home and wanted to give Wedgwood Baptist Church the proceeds of the sale to help the victims.

We met together with the family, their pastor, and the elders of their church. A few leaders plus Kevin Galey and Jeff Laster, two victims who were now out of the hospital, accompanied me.

We spoke words of love and healing. We prayed. We held hands and sang, "Blest be the tie that binds our hearts in Christian love."

The Hardest Act of Forgiveness

When life spins out of control, when the darkness descends and we are left with only the shattered pieces of our hopes and dreams, and all our "Whys?" go unanswered, most of us are confronted with the necessity to forgive God.

"How could You let my child die?"

"Couldn't You have healed his cancer?"

"Couldn't You have saved my marriage?"

The list goes on as our broken heart aches in despair. The choice must be made: to continue to wallow in paralyzing bitterness or to choose to forgive and move on, trusting in God's unfailing love.

I have lived long enough to learn how important it is to resign my position as General Manager of the Universe and let God be God. Forgiveness is a choice. Choose it or perish

THE NEED FOR CHRISTIAN COUNSELING

Sigmund Freud was one of the seminal minds of the 20th Century. Through his treatment of "Fraulein O," he discovered and theorized about the subconscious and its effects on the human personality. As such, he is known as the "Father of Modern Psychology." Though most psychologists no longer hold much of the theories of psychoanalysis, few would deny the influence of psychosomatic factors in mental and emotional health.

Freud was an ardent atheist. When it came to religion, the normally cool and careful Freud lost his calm objectivity. He was virulently opposed to religion in any form. He was convinced that teachings about God and morality were the root of all psychoses. He held that the fruit of religion was guilt, shame, and condemnation that result in mental illness.

Thus, there has come to be a general antipathy between religion in general and biblical Christianity in particular and the practitioners of psychology and professional counseling.

Evangelicals often view Psychology as the "wisdom of men" as opposed to the counsels of God. The Bible boldly claims that in Christ "are hidden all the treasures of wisdom and knowledge" (Colossians 2:3). Under the general heading of "The Sufficiency of Christ," they insist that biblically knowledgeable Christians have been granted "everything pertaining to life and godliness" (2 Peter 1:3). Any usage of extra-biblical theories or practices is often viewed as deadly compromise with the false wisdom of this world.

In recent years, this mutual animosity has been deepened by the so-called "Culture Wars" between the Evangelical world and modern secular Humanism. While the scientific community often views biblical Christians as Neanderthal superstitionists, Evangelicals see themselves as standing firmly against the worldview of godless scholarship. They almost revel in the scorn heaped upon them as an example of the "foolishness of God (that) is wiser than men..." (1 Corinthians 1:25).

The Need for Balance

It is often sound advice to step back for a bit and try to take a balanced approach. When there appears to be conflict between the Bible and science, it is usually because the Bible has been misinterpreted or because science has been misunderstood. God is the Author of both Scripture, which He inspired, and science, which He created. With a common, infallible Source, there can be no inherent incongruities.

One tenet of the Christian faith and worldview that is often ignored is that "All truth is God's truth." God is both the Source and Foundation of all wisdom and knowledge according to the book of Proverbs. If one discovers how plants grow or the liver functions, whether the discoverer is a believer or not, the discovery is a result of what our Puritan forefathers called "Common Grace." That is, God bestows blessings on the just and the unjust alike (Matthew 5:45). The rain falls on the land of the Christian and the non-Christian.

Consequently, even nonbelieving people can compose a beautiful symphony, write a compelling poem, and have the expertise to fix a broken washing machine, possess moral character, or be a faithful husband and father. And, unbelieving scientists can discover truths about God's creation that may not have been revealed in the special revelation we know as Scripture but are true and enlightening, nevertheless.

While God's special revelation in the Bible does give us all we need for life and godliness, it does not provide insight as to how to deal with an engine knock in your automobile or to treat prostate cancer or to invest your money.

For these questions, we go to people who have spent their lives in those fields of endeavor, and we trust those who have a track record of success, regardless of their religious persuasion.

While the vast majority of our psychological and emotional issues can be dealt with by applying scriptural principles to the problems of our life, we would be remiss if we refuse the help of people who have been trained, not only in biblical theology but also in counseling techniques and practice.

Beyond that, there are some mental disorders that have their root in physical causes. Sometimes, chemical prescriptions are needed to counteract imbalances in the blood and glandular systems in our bodies. One understands that it is God who is the Source of that chemical discovery and that "every perfect gift is from above, coming down from the Father of lights..." (James 1:17). We seek the insight of psychiatrists and medical doctors who are knowledgeable in these matters. To reject these resources as the "wisdom of this world" is to fail to avail ourselves of the blessings that God's common grace has provided. I am grateful for the polio vaccine, regardless of Jonas Salk's religious convictions.

Barb's Story

My oldest sister, Barbara, was having difficulty adjusting to life after high school. She was attending junior college while living at home. She was chafing under the rules of the house laid down by my father that conflicted with her sense of newfound independence.

The conflict between my sister and my father grew in intensity until one day my sisters and I came home to an empty house with a tear-stained note from my mother. She explained that Barb had had a "nervous breakdown" and the college officials had placed her in a local hospital. She was eventually diagnosed with "paranoid schizophrenia," although they did not know much about that illness or how to treat it.

Unfortunately, after several rounds of electric shock therapy and counseling, Barb's doctors insisted her first step to mental health meant rejecting all those "archaic concepts about God and the Bible" that she had learned from her parents and youth leaders.

My sister was nothing if she was not stubborn. She told her psychiatrists that she would die in a mental hospital before she would give up her faith! And so, the doctors told my parents she would never be sane again and to just place her in the state mental asylum and "throw away the key!" (I am not making this up.)

My parents simply could not bring themselves to make that awful decision. The result was nearly 40 years of emotional extremes, from seasons of lethargy and weight loss to times of suicidal depression and obesity. Eventually, Barb refused all psychiatric care, as only electroshock therapy had had any effect upon her. Unfortunately, it also left her in a mental and emotional stupor. The last time she used the prescribed medicine, she experienced an adverse reaction, and Barb tried to take her life by swallowing the entire bottle of pills.

For decades, my parents lived in fear of a phone call in the middle of the night informing them that Barb had been found dead in an alleyway or that her apartment had burned down around her. I would visit with her during my annual visits to my home in Michigan, but it was only a matter of minutes before the conversation turned to rage and spiraled out of control.

In the past 50 years, researchers have discovered that schizophrenia occurs primarily in young women between the ages of 18 and 25. It is caused not by archaic religious views but by a lack of serotonin in the bloodstream and thinness in the nerve connections between synapses in the brain.

For decades, Barb cycled between bouts of rage and bitterness and deep, paralyzing depression. Then, one day, after her bedding had caught fire (the third time in a month) from the cigarettes she smoked incessantly, the Fire Marshall had her hospitalized for being a danger to herself and others.

"Oh, Albie," she cried to me. "They've taken the last thing I had: my freedom!"

But since her last time in the hospital, 20 years ago, scientists had, thankfully, discovered new medicines that could replace the much-needed serotonin in her bloodstream. The new medicines seemed to work!

And, I got my sister back for the last few years of her life before she finally died of cancer.

Faith Community and Trauma Recovery

Our experiences after the Wedgwood shooting were vastly helped by the participation of the Counseling community. We were blessed to have the resources of the Counseling department of Southwestern Baptist Theological Seminary close by, and we availed ourselves of that resource with regularity.

Immediately after the shooting, Dr. Scott Floyd and Dr. Ian Jones made themselves and their counseling students available to us. Many of their students and graduates were members of our church. They were there at the church in the chaotic aftermath and at the funerals that soon followed. They were there with our youth that Tuesday night when students were encouraged to express their feelings on the concrete floor of the church. They continued to offer their counsel for the years to follow as Post Traumatic Stress Disorder began to appear in the lives of church members and first responders.

I insisted that every staff member of our church get counseling, and as an example, my wife and I went to counseling and benefitted thereby.

At that time, mass shootings, especially in churches, were so unprecedented that communities were unprepared to know how to respond. One local high school administrator actually insisted that students not be allowed to talk about it at all as it was now (just a few days later) "time to move on"!

Recent studies by the Humanitarian Disaster Institute (HDI), as revealed in a presentation to the American Psychological Association, explained that people who availed themselves of the support offered by religious communities experienced fewer symptoms of depression and Post Traumatic Stress Disorder.[5] Even secular sources admit that a strong faith is of great benefit in weathering catastrophic trauma.

Christian Counseling

It is apparent that the support that a faith community provides, coupled with sensitive and practical counselors who share the same biblical perspective, is the optimum way to deal with the grief and loss that mass tragedies create.

Christian Counseling is rooted in at least three tenets:

1. *The Authority of God's Word*
    While God has revealed truths that transcend scriptural teachings, no truth claims should contradict what is clearly taught in the Bible. God cannot contradict Himself.

2. *Trained Listeners*
    Counseling is primarily the art of insightful listening. Healing comes, not in the dispensing of one's own wisdom but in the talking out of one's trauma coupled with God-given insight in the process.

    The gift of discerning listening can be developed through practice and experience. "The hearing ear and the seeing eye, the Lord has made both of them" (Proverbs 20:12).

---

[5] https://www.theaquilareport.com/researchers-faith-helps-mass-shooting-survivors/

3. *Knowing When to Refer*

Finally, even the most trained counselor knows when to refer the client to those with experience and training that go beyond their own. This is especially true when it comes to prescribing medication.

Dr. Scott Floyd has recently published a book, *Crisis Counseling*, in which he describes intervention strategies in matters of trauma, stress, and crisis. He explains the differences in dealing with children, adolescents, and adults. Much of his material arose out of his experiences in helping with the aftermath of the Wedgwood shooting. I recommend it highly.

One thing is clear. When trauma of this magnitude occurs, we do well to make use of all the resources God has provided for us. Both the prayers and presence of loved ones and church members combined with the patient and Spirit-led help of the Counseling Community are necessary in recovering from shock and crisis like ours.

As a pastor, I do not know what I would have done without all the help God granted us during this crucial time in our lives.

DEALING WITH DEPRESSION

O ne of the most devastating effects of trauma such as we have experienced is deep, lasting, debilitating depression.

Depression is so widespread, it has been referred to as "the common cold of mental illness." According to the American Psychological Association (APA), depression affects one in every 15 American adults every year (6.7 percent). One in six of all-American adults (16.6 percent) will experience significant depression at one time or another in their lifetime. Women are twice as likely to suffer from its debilitating effects.

Depression affects how one feels and acts. It can lead to a variety of physical and emotional problems and decrease one's ability to function. Some of these effects are feeling sadness, loss of interest, changes in appetite, sleeping disorders, loss of energy, feeling worthless or guilty, difficulty thinking or making decisions, and compelling thoughts about death or suicide. Left unaddressed, depression can lead to self-harm and even the taking of one's life.

After the shooting at Wedgwood in 1999, I experienced these symptoms myself and counseled with those who had also suffered these manifestations.

According to the APA, chronic depression must last at least two weeks to qualify as such.[6] Shorter bouts of sadness and grief are the natural results of trauma and crisis, and as such, are to be expected as an appropriate way for the mind and body to call "timeout" in order to deal with the issues. But, when

---

[6] https://www.psychiatry.org/patients-families/depression/what-is-depression

the depression continues and deepens, it becomes chronic and must be dealt with carefully and skillfully.

Various Factors in Depression

There are several different causes behind chronic depression, each of which requires individual and specific treatment. As we have seen, one of the causes is shocking, tragic experiences. Some of these experiences are sudden, like violence or sudden death of a loved one. Others are more long-term, such as ongoing abuse, neglect, or extreme poverty.

Depression can also arise out of personal issues, such as low self-esteem or a long-standing pessimism. Recent studies have found that genetics play a factor. Depression has been found to run in families.

Finally, biochemistry can also be a causal factor. Lack of certain chemicals in the bloodstream or nerve endings in the brain is known to contribute to emotional illness and depression.

The Shame Factor

Sadly, evangelical Christians have tended to view depression as a function of sin. It is wrongfully believed that a very depressed spirit is antithetical to the joyful, abundant life that Jesus promises to those who abide in Him (John 10:10).

Some of the songs we sing do not match up with what most of us experience.

"Every day with Jesus is sweeter than the day before..."

This is simply not true. Nor does the Bible teach it. Ephesians 6 enjoins us to "put on the whole armor of God, that you may be able to withstand in the evil day" (v. 13). Evidently, some days are more evil than others!

So, when one of us suffers with depression, what we often get from fellow church members is rebuke. "Have faith. Choose joy. Pray more. Bind Satan." What this produces is guilt and shame in addition to their depression.

Several years ago, I was asked to speak at a local conference of African American churches on the Black Church and Mental Illness. As I talked with black pastors, I was told that they did not have the freedom to share their emotional struggles because their position on the "pastoral pedestal" of emotional and spiritual maturity just would not allow it. They were forced to conceal the emotional struggle they and their family members were experiencing and to pretend to be always victorious.

Great People and Depression

Chronic depression has been a common ailment, even among the greatest figures in history. Alexander the great, after conquering Persia, literally broke down in tears because there were no more worlds to conquer. He turned to alcohol and dissipation and drank himself to death.

John Quincy Adams, an overachiever from early childhood and America's sixth president, wrote in his diary: "My life has been spent in vain and idle aspirations, and in ceaseless rejected prayers that something would be the result of my existence beneficial to my species."[7]

Abraham Lincoln never carried a gun for fear of committing suicide in a rash moment.

Winston Churchill called depression, "My little black dog."

Author Robert Louis Stevenson had written for his epitaph, "Here lies one who meant well, who tried a little, and failed much."[8]

---

[7] Donald McCullough, "The Pitfalls of Positive Thinking," *Christianity Today* (Sept. 6, 1985).
[8] Ibid.

Buzz Aldrin, one of the few astronauts who walked on the moon, was known to have said that when you achieve all your goals, you tend to become depressed. Upon returning to Earth, he broke down emotionally.

What About Christians?

It appears that the Christian faith is no guarantee against bouts of severe depression, contrary to what many might insist.

Martin Luther struggled with depression his entire life. Some of his problems were due to intestinal issues; others were due to spiritual attack. On many sleepless nights, he would mentally spar with the devil. His wife, Catherine, had to hide the knives in the house for his protection. In a letter to his colleague Melanchthon, he wrote:

"I should be afire in the spirit; in reality I am afire in the flesh, with lust, laziness, idleness, sleepiness...For the last eight days I have written nothing, nor prayed nor studied...I really cannot stand it any longer."

John Newton, the former slave trader turned preacher and hymn writer, wrote probably the most popular hymn of all: "Amazing Grace." But, he also wrote a wonderful hymn that aptly describes his struggle with depression:

"How tedious and tasteless the hours,
When Jesus no longer I see;
Sweet prospects, sweet birds and sweet flowers,
Have all lost their sweetness to me;
The midsummer sun shines but dim,
The fields strive in vain to look gay;
But when I am happy in Him,
December's as pleasant as May."

But what does one do when the cold, dark days of December befall us? Newton goes on to describe it in verse two:

"Dear Lord, if indeed I am Thine,
If Thou art my sun and my song,
Say, why do I languish and pine,
And why are my winters so long?
O drive these dark clouds from my sky,
Thy soul-cheering presence restore;
Or take me unto Thee on high,
Where winters and clouds are no more."

Obviously, Newton was plagued with thoughts of death and suicide. His friend and fellow hymn writer, William Cowper ("There Is a Fountain Filled with Blood"), struggled with suicidal depression all his life. On a number of occasions, he tried but failed to take his life. He swallowed poison but vomited it back up. He tried hanging himself, but the rope broke. He stabbed himself, but the blade snapped! Today, Cowper would likely be diagnosed as a paranoid schizophrenic.

Bible Heroes and Depression

The Bible itself describes a number of saints who struggled with suicidal depression in transparent and graphic terms.

Cain: When <u>Anger</u> Leads to Depression

The ugly specter of deep depression occurs early in Scripture with the first man born to human parents: Cain. In Genesis 4, we read the well-known account of Cain and Abel. Abel's offering was acceptable to God because he brought the best of his flocks for a blood offering, while Cain's offering was only the leftovers of his crop, and it did not involve a blood sacrifice. Cain's response to God's rejection was black anger and dark depression. The Word says, "his countenance fell" (v. 5), a Hebrew idiom describing emotional despondency. God chastises him and tells him if he would do well, his "countenance (will) be lifted up" (v. 7). But Cain chose to act wickedly out of a depressed spirit, and he tragically murdered his own brother.

From earliest times, observers have noted the close connection between anger and depression. Anger, when it is not dealt with, can easily lead to deep depression. Anger itself is not a sin. Indeed, even God is described as angry many times, but His is a righteous anger.

The Bible tells us, "Be ye angry, and sin not: let not the sun go down upon your wrath" (Ephesians 4:26). It is when anger is left to smolder, when it goes unaddressed and unresolved, that it turns to sin and, eventually, depression. As God warns Cain, an angry heart finds that sin is "crouching at your door" (Genesis 4:7).

Job: When Tragedy Strikes

One of the most descriptive accounts of chronic depression in the Bible is the case of ancient Job, whom God Himself describes as, "a blameless and upright man fearing God and turning away from evil" (Job 2:3). The Scripture is clear that Job's trials and subsequent depression were not a result of his own sin and shortcomings. It is clear, depression itself is not a sin in God's eyes; it is how we respond to it, what actions we take as a result. Emotions in themselves are not wrong; they just are. Nowhere are we commanded to feel anything, but we are not to let our emotions determine our actions.

Job's activities are a perfect description of classic depression. He tries to withdraw from society: "Leave me alone!" he tells his friends (Job 7:19). He ceases all activity, sitting among the ashes (2:8). He cannot pray (implied throughout the book). He curses the day he was born (3:1). He longs for death (3:21).

The cause behind Job's despair is life-shaking tragedy. He loses all his flocks and herds. All of his children are suddenly destroyed. His wealth dissipates. And then his health is gone. His reputation as a godly man is even ruined as his friends conclude that he must be some kind of vile sinner, suffering the chastening of Almighty God.

Without his health, his wealth, his children, or his friends, all Job is left with is unrelenting pain and a wife who tells him to curse God and die.

All this occurs in spite of him being "a blameless and upright man."

Moses: When <u>Overwork</u> Results in Despair

Moses was perhaps the greatest leader in human history. Consider the unimaginable task of first getting the Egyptians to let three million slaves go free. These were the slaves who built the pyramids, who were the backbone of Egypt's economy and the cause of their fantastic wealth! Consider galvanizing three million semi-educated, grumbling, discontented, just-emerging-from-the-Bronze-Age malcontents into a nation. Then, consider trying to lead them through some of the most God-forsaken deserts in the world. This is a job description that no one in his right mind would ever take on.

Moses was a type A, overachieving "alpha dog" with a perfectionist bent. Who else could be trusted with all the minute details of the Tabernacle? Who else could be the one to whom Jehovah God could reveal His Law and then teach it to the original "school for slow learners"?

All the responsibilities of the legislative, judicial, and executive branches of government fell into Moses's lap. He collapsed under the weight of it all!

In Numbers 11, we have the account of Moses' nervous breakdown:

"It is too burdensome for me," he laments. "Please kill me at once, if I have found favor in Your sight" (vs. 14, 15). In other words, "Do me a favor, God—kill me right here and now!" Moses is clearly suicidal in his depression.

The answer, so obvious to us with the benefit of hindsight, is to divide the labor. Find people you can trust to handle the lesser problems. Multiply the workforce and share the workload with others.

But notice that God does not chide his servant for his depression.

David: Hopelessness and Depression

David was known not only as the shepherd boy who brought down the giant Goliath but also as the warrior king who established the kingdom and the royal line of Messiah. The "sweet psalmist of Israel" (2 Samuel 23:1) seemed to have it all together, going from one triumph to another. But, it all came crashing down when, in his 70s after 40 years of successful rule, his charismatic son, Absalom, rose in rebellion against him. Forced to flee from the capital, Jerusalem, he and his ragtag remnant stole through the Judean desert, running for their lives. Along the way, Shimei, a descendant of the former King Saul, hurled dust, dirt, stones, and curses upon him. This was not exactly the way King David envisioned his career winding down.

With his own son in rebellion, his people rejecting his leadership, and running through the desert for his life like a whipped puppy, David longed for the good old days when he led the procession into the House of the Lord on national feast days.

In Psalm 41 and again in chapter 42, David speaks of his continual tears "day and night," his longing for God, his deep depression because of the oppression of his enemies who mock him.

In the depths of his darkness and hopelessness, David talks to himself, reminding himself to hope in God, no matter how hopeless the circumstances.

Elijah: When Loneliness and Exhaustion Lead to Depression

The Bible portrays its heroes in realistic tones, refusing to ignore or gloss over people's faults or weaknesses. James describes the prophet Elijah as a man with a nature like ours (James 5:17). Yet, he too came to a place in his life where depression made him long for death.

After hiding in the wilderness during a severe drought that he had boldly predicted, and after being fed daily by ravens and then by a Gentile widow, Elijah finally challenged the prophets of Baal to a public contest to determine whether Baal or Jehovah was the One True God.

The lone prophet won the contest hands-down, and then he called down the first rainstorm in three-and-a-half years, at the beginning of the dry season, no less! But, when he finally arrived at home, a message came from the evil Queen Jezebel that threatened his very life.

Filled with terror, the man of God who single-handedly defeated 450 prophets of Baal, ran for his life! Leaving his servant in the dust, he fled into the Negev Desert and prayed that he might die. Exhausted, hungry, thirsty, disappointed, and horribly alone, Elijah was overwhelmed with suicidal depression.

The factors behind his despair were multitudinous. Physically, his body was hungry, thirsty, and utterly worn out. Emotionally, he was filled with the wild terror and a sense of cosmic isolation: "I am the only one left," he complained to God (1 Kings 19:10). Spiritually, Elijah was gripped with guilt, having run from a wicked woman so shortly after his triumph on Mount Carmel. His pride was deeply wounded as he admitted, "I am no better than my fathers!" (v. 4). Who ever told him he was?

Convinced his life was hopelessly in ruins, Elijah pled with God to take his life.

How tenderly God dealt with his broken servant!

To address Elijah's physical needs, God granted him sleep. He provided a jar of cool water to slake his thirst. And then some "angel food cake" appeared, still warm from the coals. After eating and drinking, Elijah lay down again for more sleep and rest.

Then, God attended to his servant's emotional needs. For his fear, God demonstrated His divine power in the wind, the earthquake, and the fire. And for his isolation, God informed him that there were still 7,000 faithful prophets who had not bowed down to Baal. And, beyond all this, God had chosen a man to be Elijah's personal servant and mentee as well as to be a companion to offset his loneliness.

Finally, to deal with Elijah's guilt and shame, He sent him on a divine journey to find his helper and anoint a king. God was not finished with him yet. He still had a purpose for his life.

Jonah: When <u>Disappointment</u> Leads to Depression

Proverbs 13:12 tells us, "Hope deferred makes the heart sick." It is when our expectations are disappointed, when our dreams are shattered and our longings go unfulfilled, that depression grips our soul.

The Prophet Jonah lived in the northern part of Israel when the Assyrians were on the rise politically and militarily. They had led the way in the development of iron against the bronze weapons of the day. Because of this technological advantage as well as their cruel ferocity, they seemed to be invincible. These sworn enemies of God's chosen people loomed on the horizon like the angel of death.

So, it is little wonder that Jonah balked at the divine call to preach a revival in the great city of Nineveh, Assyria's impregnable capital! He had been praying daily for the destruction of the Ninevites, and now God was asking Jonah to preach truth to them and rescue them from their spiritual blindness.

After foolishly trying to run from an omnipresent God, Jonah finally "washed up" on the outskirts of the great city. Reluctantly, but obediently, he preached an eight-word sermon: "Yet forty days, and Nineveh shall be overthrown!" (Jonah 3:4).

No deathbed illustrations. No word studies. No praise band playing softly during the invitation. Eight words and revival broke out in the wicked city of Nineveh.

And the prophet was heartbroken, depressed, sulking, and suicidal! "It is better for me to die than to live," he complained (4:3).

Notice the classic symptoms of debilitating depression. He withdrew from society on a hill outside the city. He gave in to inactivity as he sat down, waiting in bitter disappointment.

Rather than providing a shallow pep talk, rather than scorching condemnation, God sent a plant, a sapling, to provide shade for the angry, disappointed man. The next day, God sent a worm to destroy the sapling and take away the shade. And then, He brought a hot east wind to increase Jonah's woes! Sometimes, things have to get worse before they get better!

But notice the sovereign control God has over the wind, the worms, the plants, the fish of the seas, and the hearts of the heathen.

Finally, as Jonah grieved despairingly over the loss of his shade tree, God pointed out his callous unconcern for the 120,000 human beings of Nineveh, not to mention their animals.

In other words, as long as our chief focus is upon ourselves, we will be at the mercy of the changing circumstances of life and unable to shake off the gloom and the disappointment that paralyzes us.

Those who struggle most with depression tend to be the most self-absorbed.

Timothy: When **Fear** Leads to Depression

Young Timothy was the Apostle Paul's "Son in the Faith." He had been converted under Paul's ministry on the first missionary journey in the city of

Lystra. Later, Paul took Timothy along with him on further church-planting trips, discipling and mentoring him.

Timothy appeared to have a timid disposition, either naturally or because of his youthful age at a time when the elderly were respected. He evidently had stomach problems and was prone to being fearful.

After investing more than three years in the church at Ephesus, Paul moved on but left Timothy in charge as their pastor. At that time, Paul began writing his final epistle. He was imprisoned in the infamous Mamertine Prison, waiting for what would eventually be a death sentence from the Emperor Nero.

The Apostle Paul reminded his young friend, "For God has not given us a spirit of fear, but of power and of love and of a sound mind" (2 Timothy 1:7).

The New Testament has three words for *fear*, but the one used here is unique. It means cowardice or terror. Fear left unchecked can lead to paralysis and deep depression. Fear actually creates what it fears. The skier who is afraid of falling falls! The student who is terrified of failing the test fails!

After Karl Wallenda fell to his death from the high wire, his wife remarked that she knew it was going to happen. In spite of a lifetime balancing on the wire above the crowds, for the last several months, he had become obsessed with falling. In an interview following his fall, his wife remarked, "All Karl thought about for three straight months prior to it was falling."[9]

How do you counter a spirit of fear?

First, remind yourself of God's unlimited power (dunamis). Paul reminded Timothy of his roots, his godly mother and grandmother, and of his calling and gifting by Almighty God.

---

[9] http://info.shine.com/article/afraid-of-falling-or-failing/786.html

Second, recall God's unconditional love. What does love have to do with combatting fear and terror? The main cause of a spirit of fear is self-concern, self-protection, and self-absorption. The best way to overcome fear and depression is to get lost in serving God and loving others. That is what John means when he says, "Perfect love casts out fear" (1 John 4:18).

Finally, you conquer fear with a sound mind: literally, sanity, control, and balance.

William Cowper, the 18th Century hymn writer who struggled all his life with mental illness, could only find comfort and peace in the sovereignty of God. When he could not find answers to the issues of life, he continued to trust in the loving grace of a sovereign God. He wrote:

"God moves in a mysterious way, His wonders to perform;
He plants His footsteps in the sea And rides upon the storm...
Ye fearful saints, fresh courage take; The clouds ye so much dread
Are big with mercy and shall break In blessings on your head.
Judge not the Lord by feeble sense, But trust Him for His grace;
Behind a frowning providence He hides a smiling face."

After the shooting at Wedgwood, depression reared its ugly head time and time again. All these factors—fear, overwork, loneliness, disappointment, anger, and, of course, deep tragedy—served to plunge many of us into prolonged periods of depression.

Rather than pretend that everything was just fine and suffer in silence, we talked openly about depression. I preached a sermon series on "Dealing with Depression," using the scriptural examples I have here explained. It has been well said, "The devil loves a secret." As long as we keep our struggles secret, we cannot find healing. We continue to wallow in despondency and shame.

Depression needs to be acknowledged, discussed, and dealt with in the light of God's healing and enlightening Word by the body of Christ as we tenderly "weep with those who weep" (Romans 12:15).

We do not have to suffer alone and in silence the paralyzing effects of depression. As an old hymn by Thomas Moore encourages us:

"Come, ye disconsolate, where'er ye languish;
Come to the mercy seat, fervently kneel;
Here bring your wounded hearts, here tell your anguish,
Earth has no sorrow that heaven cannot heal."

THE ISSUE OF SECURITY

Columbine, Wedgwood, Aurora, Sandy Hook, San Bernardino, Orlando, Las Vegas, Charleston, Sutherland Springs...the list of mass shootings in schools, venues, churches, and night clubs seems to grow like a cancer in our society. As one shock after another occurs, we seem to be growing more and more callous to the horrors. One after another, each massacre soon becomes yesterday's news and is soon forgotten.

In light of this tragic trend, one of our nation's growth industries has become the issue of Security. Training sessions, seminars, and books have been dedicated to this sobering reality. The issue of public security is a hot one. I have been told that this is the subject I should write about if I want to write a best-seller, especially regarding smaller churches, businesses, and institutions.

It is with great reluctance that I devote a chapter on this issue. I am not an expert on this subject, despite having attended and spoken at several conferences dedicated to the question of security. I am well aware that my views and convictions fly in the face of those of the vast majority of Americans and evangelicals. Some of my dearest friends have become exceedingly angry with me over this. A few even left our church in anger and disappointment.

Although I see no benefit in stirring up needless strife and conflict in the body of Christ, I am keenly aware that a man-pleasing spirit is a guarantee of the forfeiture of the blessing of God. As William Cowper writes: "Fear Him, ye saints, and you will then have nothing else to fear...."

And so, I share what I believe God has taught us regarding the crucial issue of Church Security.

Practical Considerations

There are many practical steps that are incumbent upon leaders to take in order to provide a modicum of safety for those under their watch care. One of the responsibilities of Pastors (Shepherds) is not only to feed the flock but also to protect it. Although my personality involves an aversion to details, I have learned that "the devil is in the details." So, I am blessed to be surrounded by people who pay attention to details for the general well-being of the body.

At Wedgwood Baptist Church, this responsibility has fallen to the Administrative team. They attend to the need for insurance, something every church or business cannot do without in this day and age. Faith in God is no substitute for taking practical steps to protect your organization.

Fire alarms are absolute necessities that are required by law.

Adequate lighting has prevented many a crime.

Security cameras are a known deterrent. At least one church gunman admitted to changing his tactics because his first target had security cameras at the entrances.

It is far more likely that a sexual predator rather than an armed gunman will target a church. The law requires comprehensive background checks for any who work with children or adolescents. Churches are among the most vulnerable objects of intention for predators in our society. All those who work with the young must be trained in spotting signs of abuse and responding appropriately. Although forgiveness is essential to the practice of our faith, we must never let Christian mercy trump the need to protect our children.

Detailed plans and practice of those plans should be laid out for responding to tragic events like fire, tornadoes, hurricanes, and, unfortunately, mass shootings.

Security teams should be recruited carefully and wisely and should be trained to respond appropriately to various threats. This is not a place for every self-appointed cowboy with a license to carry permit who wants to demonstrate his manliness. These should be people of insight. The goal is to prevent violence, not engender it. When traumatic events threaten, they should be adept at talking down the disturbed perpetrator, not inciting him.

In all the various places and churches where I have spoken, the best example of effective security I have found is at First Baptist Church of Fort Lauderdale, Florida. Their leader, Wiley Thompson, brings a lifetime of experience in law enforcement into play. First Baptist is a downtown church with all the issues that brings to bear. They told me of their "finest hour" when, on a Wednesday evening while the church swarmed with activity, a homeless man, having just burglarized a local store, fled from police into the church. In a matter of minutes, their security team located the fugitive, disarmed him, and presented him to the police. The best thing about the whole affair was that no one attending church knew anything bad had happened!

It is an obvious fact that few churches have the resources of First Baptist Church, Fort Lauderdale. Nevertheless, even smaller churches can invest in cameras and lighting. There are laypeople in every congregation who are gifted in administration who could develop action plans. Denominational support for security training is available to many. Conferences and plan books are also available to anyone interested.

There is no excuse for failure to take practical steps to protect those given to our charge. As the old saying goes, "Forewarned is forearmed."

Good Guys with Guns?

The proliferation of handguns and automatic rifles in America is completely and astonishingly unprecedented. There are more than 300 million handguns in the United States, one for every man, woman, boy, and girl. In the name of the constitutionally protected "right to bear arms," assault rifles and automatic handguns proliferate within our population. Let us be clear, these weapons are not made for hunting wild game; they are designed for shooting people.

The World Health Organization reports that gun homicide rates range from zero deaths per million in United Kingdom to five in Canada. No other industrialized country comes close to the United States' rate of 36 per million.[10] Clearly, America has a gun violence problem.

People in other modern industrialized nations are astounded by the violence that pervades the United States as a result. The most common defense of this situation is that of self-protection. An old bumper sticker says, "When guns are outlawed, only outlaws will have guns."

And so, the carnage continues. Although the United States only comprises less than five percent of the world's population, almost three percent of the world's shooting incidents occur in America.[11] Americans who own firearms are twice the number, percentage wise, of that in other countries.[12]

The National Crime Victimization Survey reported in 2013 that, in the United States in 99.2 percent of violent attacks, no gun is ever used for defensive purposes.[13]

---

[10] https://www.cbsnews.com/news/how-u-s-gun-deaths-compare-to-other-countries/

[11] https://econjwatch.org/articles/is-the-united-states-an-outlier-in-public-mass-shootings-a-comment-on-adam-lankford

[12] https://www.worldatlas.com/articles/countries-with-the-highest-rate-of-gun-ownership.html

[13] https://www.futurity.org/crime-guns-laws-1465992-2/

Every time there is another shocking mass shooting, gun sales go UP appreciably as Americans fear their ability to arm themselves might be curtailed in some way.

In 2017, a Stanford University study investigated the effect of states passing right-to-carry (handgun) laws on violent crime rates during the following 10 years. Stanford law professor John Donohue found that in the 33 states that passed right-to-carry laws, rates of violent crimes rose 13 to 15 percent over states that did not adopt those laws. He went on to conclude that those states would have to double their prison population in order to counter the effects of right-to-carry laws on violent crime.[14]

The danger I see in bringing concealed weapons into our churches is a shoot-out mentality that threatens to result in even more violence.

Dangers in Profiling

How do we know whom to shoot? Do we place armed guards at the door to profile, frisk, or bar "undesirables" who might be a threat to our congregation?

In the weeks following the shooting at Wedgwood, we were nervous and tense as we gathered together, as one might expect. One Sunday night, a stranger walked in covered with tattoos, having a shaved head, and wearing a tank top. Everyone held his or her breath in fear. But, as the music started, he got up and ran out. We all breathed a sigh of relief.

The next Sunday evening, he showed up a second time. Yet again, the anxiety level spiked. The man was obviously troubled, but once the sermon started, he ran out again. At that time, we felt as though God had "protected us" once again.

---

[14] Cook, Philip J., and John J. Donohue. "Saving Lives by Regulating Guns: Evidence for Policy." *Science*, Dec 8, 2017.

The third Sunday night, he came back and made it through the entire service. After the message, when the invitation was given, he came forward and shared that he had violated his parole and was soon headed back to prison. He realized he could not survive there without Christ. He was born again and baptized in the next week.

What if we would have had guards at the entrances to screen out folks like that? Are these not the very ones we should reach? In the interest of church security, is there not a danger of turning our sanctuaries into fortresses to isolate "the frozen chosen" from the ones we are called to evangelize?

I do not know what can be done about the violence that pervades our nation. There is little realistic hope that the gun lobby that controls Congress will ever allow significant restraints on the sale of weapons or that the American people, as a whole, favor those restraints.

I do know this: Scripture tells us that those who trust in chariots (or weapons) are foolish and doomed. Our security lies ultimately in God Himself. He is our Shield and Protector. Our church doors should remain open to the hurting and needy.

Wise preparation and plans should be made, but not from an attitude of paranoia. Take reasonable steps but avoid a spirit of panic.

Keep the doors open. Be vigilant. Fear not.

And trust God.

THE MESSAGE OF HOPE

Some years ago, off the coast of Massachusetts, a submarine was mistakenly rammed by another ship, and it sunk like a stone to the bottom of the cold Atlantic. A few survivors had locked themselves in a compartment and waited for rescue. The sub had sunk so rapidly, they wondered whether or not a "Mayday" had even been sent out.

So, they waited desperately as their air supply slowly ran out.

Fortunately, the call for help was received, and the Coast Guard sent out a rescue team to search for survivors. Rescue workers descended to the sunken ship, and as they approached, they heard a strange tapping sound from within. Sending the joyous news that there were indeed survivors, they redoubled their rescue attempt.

Then, one of the rescuers recognized that the tapping sound was Morse code. What was the frantic message of those trapped in the submarine?

"Is...there...any...hope?"

It strikes me that this is the desperate cry of our generation. The 20th Century proved to be the bloodiest century in the long and bellicose history of mankind. Two world wars took the lives of more than 60 million people. Two whole generations have been lost forever.

What can be said for a society that has given us the Holocaust, gas and nerve warfare, firebombing and napalm, Hiroshima and Nagasaki? What can be said to explain Ypres, the Somme, Auschwitz, Stalingrad, Mỹ Lai, and Hamburger Hill? Declared wars between nations have given way to general conflict between cultures as Wahhabi Muslim terrorism threatens the very survival of our species. That is, if our rape of the planet's ecosystem doesn't finish us off first, as politicians under the well-paid control of fossil fuel industrialists deny the very existence of an ecological problem!

Cultural Hopelessness

In literature and drama, the result has been the "Theatre of the Absurd."

In Samuel Beckett's play, "Waiting for Godot," two characters sit on a bench waiting for Godot to arrive. The conversation never rises above the level of utter banalities, and Godot never arrives!

Philosophically, this absurd viewpoint is expressed in Existentialism, an anti-philosophy that insists one can never ascertain any sense or meaning to life. There are no answers, merely absurd existence in the light of one's inescapable death. Albert Camus likens man's condition to that of Sisyphus who, according to Greek mythology, was condemned by the gods to roll a huge boulder up a steep incline, trying not to get crushed in the process, only to have it roll back down again and to repeat the endless struggle once more.

In classical music, Arnold Schoenberg produced discordant sounds of music written without a key, without a foundation to arrange a melody and harmony. The resultant noise has the same effect as a fingernail being dragged across the blackboard. Atonal music is the audible expression of a culture that has lost its moorings.

In popular music, we have descended into the banal wailings of Country and Western tunes about long-haul truckers, prison blues, and infidelity, yet nostalgically longing for a time when values were secure and answers were readily available. This is accompanied by the rhythmic but rash beats of rap music that seems to extol violence and perverted sex.

In society, students at the University of California during the 1960's marched on the Administration Building singing the old civil rights song, "We Shall Overcome," but they changed the words to, "We are all insane." Suicide has become one of the leading causes of death among young and old alike.

Politics has degenerated into uncivil partisanship where those elected represent special interest groups that cannot agree on the time of day. Congressional representatives are locked in the hip pocket of lobbyists representing the wealthy few. Fewer and fewer citizens even bother to cast their ballots.

Increasingly, our generation is drawing Nietzsche's conclusion that "God is dead, and we have killed Him." Modern man no longer has a need for God. Darwin explained how nature came about and progresses; Marx explained how History develops; finally, Freud explained how the human soul operates.

Who, then, needs God?

The first and most searching question I was confronted with after the shooting at Wedgwood was, "Where was God in all this?"

It Could Have Been Worse

It was only after the initial shock was over and we looked back that we realized how much more devastating the shooting at Wedgwood could have been. Ashbrook had armed himself with no less than 200 rounds of ammunition as well as a pipe bomb. There were at least 500 young people in the pews on the lower level of the sanctuary. It was like fish in a barrel.

Many of the students were convinced it was merely a skit. These would jump up from beneath the pews and shout, "I believe in Jesus! Shoot me!" Then, they would dive back under the seat, frustrating the assailant even more.

Mary Beth Talley had been out in the foyer with those manning the table selling CDs. As the shooter made his way down the hallway, Mary Beth ran inside to warn her friends about the impending peril. In the back row was the sister of one of her friends, Heather MacDonald, an 18-year-old with Down syndrome. Disliking enclosed spaces, Heather refused to get under the pew despite her mother's pleas. Mary Beth quickly draped her body over Heather's to shield her while the gunman entered the sanctuary. Looking down, he shot Mary Beth in the back at point blank range.

When I arrived at the scene, the first victim's name our Youth Minister, Jay Fannin, told me of was Mary Beth. I wondered how I would be able to tell her single-parent mom that her only child was no longer with us.

But Mary Beth was not dead. Ashbrook had packed many of the bullets himself with varying degrees of powder. Some bullets went through walls and doors. Others had little penetrating power at all. The bullet penetrated her back but stopped short of reaching her spine or vital organs. In fact, because she was afflicted with scoliosis (curvature of the spine), the bullet entered her back where her spine should have been...but it missed! She was released from the hospital the next day.

It could have been worse.

As the students refused to take him seriously, Ashbrook grew increasingly frustrated. A video taken by a seminary wife that was subsequently destroyed showed him pacing angrily back and forth across the back of the auditorium. Finally, noticing the camerawoman at the front, he shot at and narrowly missed her. In a rage, he then lit the pipe bomb and hurled it at her.

Had the bomb landed in the crowd, there would've easily been scores of casualties. But the bomb rolled to the front of the church and was stopped by a wall. Had it exploded outwardly, dozens of students would have been hit. But it exploded upwardly, and the shrapnel landed in the balcony where only the soundman sat.

It could have been so much worse.

If Jeremiah Neitz had not confronted him so soon after the shooting began, who knows how many more would have been killed or wounded.

It could have been worse.

The Source of Our Hope

Romans 15:13 has become especially meaningful to us in subsequent years:

"Now may the God of hope fill you with all joy and peace in believing, that you may abound in hope by the power of the Holy Spirit."

Let us examine this wonderful verse more closely.

WHEN: "Now"

Someone has well said that we serve an on-time God. He is never too early or too late. His grace arrives at just the moment when we need it most.

Corrie ten Boom, the Dutch spinster whose family was imprisoned in a Nazi concentration camp for sheltering Jews, was terrified at the time of their arrest. She remembered her father's words from her childhood as she wondered how they would ever endure the horrors to come:

"Father sat down on the edge of the narrow bed. 'Corrie,' he began gently, 'when you and I go to Amsterdam—when do I give you your ticket?'

I sniffed a few times, considering this.

'Why, just before we get on the train.'

'Exactly. And our wise Father in heaven knows when we're going to need things, too. Don't run out ahead of Him, Corrie. When the time comes that some of us will have to die, you will look into your heart and find the strength you need—just in time.'"[15]

WHO: "the God of hope"

What a wonderful name for God! Be it known that the New Testament word for "hope" is not just a wishful longing for the impossible, nor is it a self-deluding whistling in the dark. Biblical hope is the sure and certain assurance, rooted in the infallible Word of God and His unfailing promises. That "blessed hope" of Christ's return is far more than Jiminy Cricket wishing on a star. It is as certain as the Incarnation and the Resurrection.

The God of hope is a rock solid, a yea and amen confidence in the darkest of times. You can be certain He is not pacing the portals of Heaven or ringing His hands in consternation as He peeks into the human condition and the mess we have made of things.

WHAT: "fill you with joy and peace"

How odd and inexplicable that genuine Christ-followers of old were not wracked with trepidation and desperation as they were being arrested, tortured, and cruelly martyred for the entertainment of the masses. There is no panic button for those whose hope and peace have its roots in the immutable God of Hope.

Christians live differently. They die differently as well.

Joy is the deep-rooted, contented confidence that, no matter the circumstances, the things that really matter—God's love and sovereign pleasure in His own—are unshakable.

Peace is not the absence of conflict but a sense of wholeness and well-being in the middle of conflict.

---

[15] Corrie ten Boom, *The Hiding Place* (Ulrichsville, OH: Barbour Publishing, Inc, 1971), 33.

These are not given sparingly, but we are full to the brim and running over with them...filled with joy and peace.

HOW: "in believing"

It is through faith that all things are possible. Apart from faith, nothing is possible. Without faith, it is impossible to please God (Hebrew 11:6). Faith mixed with love is the essence of what matters most to God (Galatians 5:6). Again, faith, like biblical hope, is not just blind wishing. It is obedience to and complete trust in a God who cannot lie. Nothing brings more glory to God than when ordinary saints choose to obey and trust God, no matter how hopeless the situation.

THE SECOND HOW: "in the power of the Holy Spirit"

It is the indwelling power of God's Holy Spirit that enables Christians to rise above their circumstances and emerge victoriously through the darkness. That is why God chooses to use the weak, the seemingly foolish, the poor "nobodies," like us at Wedgwood, so that the world will realize it is not *our* strength and character but the power of God alone that is so amazing.

WHY: "that you may abound in hope"

As the world grows darker and more hopeless, the children of God shine all the brighter. The world is desperate for the hope we have in Christ. If ever there was a time when hope was in high demand and short supply, it is now. Without hope, we are like Robinson Crusoe, stranded alone on an island, trying to scrounge up the best life we can from the wreckage of the world, living what Thoreau called "lives of quiet desperation."

What is the worst possible thing that can happen to the sincere believer? Death? What does that entail? The Apostle Paul informs us that to be absent from the body is to be present with the Lord (2 Corinthians 5:8).

As I visited with Kathy Jo Brown, whose young husband was killed that night, she asked me weepingly, "Brother Al, the Bible says God will save us from our enemies. Why didn't He save Shawn that night?" Good question!

The answer God gave me was this: The enemy's intent to destroy Shawn proved only to be God's maître d' saying, "Right this way. Your table is waiting." Shawn Brown, who loved nachos, Christian rap, baseball, and his pickup truck, was now teaching the angels rap, throwing nothing but strikes, and eating heavenly nachos with no danger of gaining weight!

In the end, no matter what happens, we win!

It is like the little boy at the pet store trying to decide which puppy to choose. They were all so cute and excitable at the prospect of going home with the lad. But there was one puppy whose exuberance was so joyful that the boy could not tell if the dog was wagging his tail or the tail was wagging the dog.

"I want the one with the happy ending," the boy said.

I do too.

HEAVEN

According to Greek mythology, humans once knew the exact date of their death. Mortality hung over their lives like the sword of Damocles. Then, Prometheus brought mankind the gift of fire, to the great displeasure of Zeus. Now, humans could reach beyond themselves and take a measure of control over their personal destiny, just like the gods. Caught up in the excitement of personal self-determination, people gradually lost the knowledge of their death day.

Our generation has lost even more. Though we are constantly reminded of the specter of death, we live in denial, choosing to exist in the eternal "Now," refusing to even consider that every biography ends with an obituary. We insist, "Elvis is alive!" We feebly try to escape the angst of Father Time, investing in health classes, Rogaine, Botox, and plastic surgery, all pathetic attempts to stave off the inevitable.

We do not even use the word "death," preferring innocuous phrases such as, "passed away" or "bought the farm" or "pushing up daisies."

When the bubonic plague first came to Europe in the 14th Century, those who could fled to the countryside. Those stricken would suffer a raging fever, oozing sores, and death within days. Those who tried to minister to them filled their pockets with flower petals to combat the stench. They would sprinkle ashes on their patients' faces, seeking to force the dying to sneeze in order to expectorate the disease. But nothing worked. Death was unavoidable. Thus, the nursery rhyme:

"Ring-a-round the roses, A pocket full of posies,
Ashes! Ashes! We all fall down."

The death rate remains 100 percent. Worldwide, two people die every second; 6,393 every hour; and 153,425 every day.[16] Psalm 90:12 reminds us, "So teach us to number our days that we may get a heart of wisdom."

The Importance of Heaven

The experience of mass shootings, where one would least expect it, demands the clarification and necessity of a robust doctrine of Heaven and eternal life.

Some have criticized the Church for being "so heavenly minded, they are no earthly good." But C.S. Lewis observed that it is precisely those who live in the shadow of eternity who end up doing the most for mankind. Those who are aware of a coming Day of Accountability are motivated to live a life of service and love. Those who realize that the final chapter of our existence is not, in Shakespeare's words, an existence "sans teeth, sans eyes, sans taste, sans everything," are the ones with the durability to press on through times of difficulty and pain.

As one old evangelist explained, "The hope of dying is the only thing that keeps me going."

One African American preacher explained it this way from an old proverb: "When you were born, you were crying while everyone else was rejoicing. So, live your life so that when you die, you are rejoicing while everyone else is crying."

Stephen Covey, in his classic book, *The Seven Habits of Highly Successful People*, noticed that successful people "begin with the end in mind." Decide what you want your loved ones to be saying about you at your funeral and then live your life to that end.

---

[16] https://www.medindia.net/patients/calculators/world-death-clock.asp

Young people are especially shocked about the sudden death of their friends. They have spent little or no time thinking about eternity. So, when death does occur suddenly, they do not know how to deal with it.

Myths About Heaven

There are many common myths about the afterlife. One of the most persistent is that it is simply a state of annihilation, where one ceases to be in any way, shape, or form. As British philosopher Bertrand Russell purported, "I believe that when I die I shall rot."[17]

From a strictly secular point of view, this seems to be a viable conclusion. Certainly, our bodily remains suffer this consequence.

However, from a psychological perspective, this is a conclusion that is untenable to most people. According to Pew Research Center's 2014 Religious Landscape Study, 72 percent of Americans still believe in Heaven in spite of the skepticism of the secularists. Indeed, 58 percent believe in Hell as well![18]

Atheistic Communism's answer to the reality of death is to encase their heroes (i.e., Lenin and Mao) in a glass vacuum, replace their blood with formaldehyde, and make a shrine of their decomposing bodies. Lenin's tomb is the most popular tourist attraction in the world. But they only prove that you cannot pump life into a dead corpse.

A second myth about Heaven is that it is inhabited by chubby nude cherubs who do nothing but sit on white puffy clouds playing harps. No wonder Mark Twain's character, Huck Finn, preferred not to spend eternity in Heaven with the likes of Aunt Sally.

---

[17] Bertrand Russell, *Why I Am Not a Christian and Other Essays on Religion and Related Subjects*, 39th ed. (Touchstone: 1967).

[18] https://www.pewresearch.org/fact-tank/2015/11/10/most-americans-believe-in-heaven-and-hell/

A third myth is that Heaven is "up there somewhere." Somewhere in outer space is some ethereal nether land where we will spend forever in endless singing. For those who are not into music, this picture leaves much to be desired.

What Heaven Is Like

Heaven is a PLACE.

In the upper room, Jesus explained that He was going to His Father's house to prepare a *place* for us. It is a place to which one can go and return. He calls it a house with many rooms that is in the process of construction (John 14:2-3).

The so-called "Lord's Prayer" does not go, "Our Father who art in a state of mind." As the first martyr, Stephen, was about to die, he saw a vision of God on His throne and Christ standing there in deep concern. Whatever Heaven is, it is a real place, and that is good news to me because death runs in my family.

In Revelation 21, however, the Apostle John has an eschatological vision in which he sees "the holy city, New Jerusalem, coming down out of heaven from God" (v. 2).

Evidently, our eternal abode will not be in outer space somewhere but in an indescribably beautiful city here on Earth—a new Earth in which God makes all things new.

Heaven is a REAL PLACE.

Heaven contains REAL PEOPLE.

Perhaps this part of the discussion should address the critical question of who is NOT in Heaven. Jesus was clear that the "broad way to destruction" was well travelled (Matthew 7:13). Jesus was no Universalist. No one spoke more about Hell than Jesus of Nazareth.

First of all, the RELIGIOUS are not found in Heaven. In the Sermon on the Mount, Jesus described the portals of Paradise where "many" remind the Judge of the Universe of all their religious accomplishments—prophecies, exorcisms, and wonders—yet are greeted with the horrendous words, "I never knew you. Depart from Me" (Matthew 7:21-23). Christ's worst condemnations were reserved for the religious leaders of His day.

Secondly, it appears manifest that the MAJORITY does not inhabit Heaven. Again, in the Sermon on the Mount, Jesus tells us, "For wide is the gate and broad is the way that leads to destruction, and there are many who go in by it" (v. 13).

Someone has well said the first thing we will ask when we get to Heaven is, "What are *you* doing here?" The second question will be, "Where is so-and-so?"

Who WILL be there?

First of all, Heaven is filled with angelic beings, far more than pudgy cherubs. These are created beings with personality, intelligence, emotions (they rejoice at the salvation of every sinner), and unbelievable power. In 2 Kings 19, we read how a single angel killed 185,000 fierce Assyrian soldiers!

Angels, by definition, are ministering creatures that not only worship God but also serve Him throughout the cosmos. They are arranged by rank and order and do battle with the forces of darkness.

Second, Heaven will be occupied by what Scripture calls The Redeemed. These come from every kindred, tribe, nation, and tongue. They are male and female, rich and poor, although there is indication that the rich and powerful will be underrepresented (1 Corinthians 1:26; Matthew 19:23). The only qualification for entrance is the admission that you do not deserve it and the simple faith that Christ died and rose again for their sake.

What will we DO?

What will we do there for eternity? Certainly, we will worship like never before in the visible presence of the Object of our worship. Ecstatic shouts and songs so loud as to dim the roar of Niagara Falls in comparison; loud instruments, trumpets, and cymbals will be part of the heavenly praise. How long all this goes on is uncertain, but one thing is clear: worship in Heaven will never be boring.

But, beyond singing and praise, we will have meaningful, purposeful, and fulfilling activities. We are told the saints will rule and reign with Christ. We will serve God there (Revelation 22:3). We will recognize one another and truly know and understand each other (1 Corinthians 13:12).

Are there pets in Heaven? Well, there are certainly animals there: lions and lambs, horses and so forth. If pets are necessary for our bliss, you can be sure God will include them.

What kind of adjectives describe Heaven?

- Joyous—outrageous joy, which is one of the key aspects
- Glorious—brightness and beauty that defies description
- New—perhaps the most repeated theme

There are two recurrent Greek words for "new" in the New Testament. One is *neos*, which has to do with chronology. The other is *bainos*, which has to do with essence or form or qualitative character. The latter is the term that the book of Revelation uses repeatedly for Heaven: New Heaven, New Earth, New Jerusalem, New song—that which is qualitatively different from the previous.

What Will NOT Be There

John relates that there will be no tears, no sorrow, no sickness, and no more death.

"Then He who sat on the throne said, 'Behold, I make all things new'" (Revelation 21:5).

There will be no sun there, for Christ Himself is the Source of light (v. 23). Nor will there be any darkness or night (v. 25).

There will be no temple in Heaven. The temple is the place were sinful man is reconciled with a sinless Creator. Sin will be banished, and the saints will be like their Savior (1 John 3:2).

Why This Chapter?

One might well ask why I would write a chapter on Heaven. What does that have to do with a book about violence, guns, and the problem of evil or forgiveness?

The fact is that the promise of Heaven gives us perspective on the sufferings, disappointments, and sorrows of this life. Death is obscene, even in its most palatable form, which hospice care can offer. One of the oldest questions of all is, "Is there life after death?"

Socrates, surrounded by his devoted disciples and about to drink the hemlock, is asked that question, and he feebly responds, "Who knows?"

Shakespeare's Hamlet contemplates suicide, asking if men would "rather bear those ills we have than fly to others we know not of?"

Job desperately asks, "When a man dies, will he live again?" (Job 14:14).

Hospitals are, in a strange way, a microcosm of life. On the surface, it appears a great place to be. It has clean sheets, warm friendly smiles everywhere, candy stripe aides seeking to make you more comfortable, the lady at the gift shop, doctors, and nurses...all smiling. Helpful. Friends and family come by with cards and flowers. The TV overhead can take you everywhere you want to go: Yankee Stadium, the White House, a cruise on the Love Boat, or a condo in Dallas.

But just when you start to relax and trust the glitzy façade, reality pierces. A siren goes off, a scream of pain emerges from a person across the hall, and then stretchers race toward the emergency room.

The truth of the matter is this: the sole purpose of the place is to bargain with death, postpone the inevitable. At best, we walk away with only an extension, never a solution to the problem.

Death is the eternal fly in the ointment of life, the lump in the carpet.

And, yet, there is one ward in the hospital where moans and cries of pain are most likely to assault your senses. Young women writhe in agony, but the staff seems oblivious to their cries, reluctant to offer sedation. Their abdomen is stretched taut; their faces wan with pain. If it were cancer, our hearts would break.

But in the maternity ward, we feel joy instead of pain. Women rarely despair. They keep the end in view. And that end—a healthy baby—causes them to endure and, later, even forget the pain.

Christians try to keep the end in view. For once, the bumper sticker is right: "Success is winding up in Heaven."

During the memorial service at the TCU stadium following the shooting, I reminded people that we had not "lost" a single person in the shooting. You have not lost something if you know exactly where it is. Scripture teaches us that, for Christians, "Absent from the body...present with the Lord" (2 Corinthians 5:8). As far as we know, every one of the victims had expressed their faith in Jesus Christ as Savior and Lord. The assurance of Heaven for all who trust in Christ is the reason we have hope and confidence in the face of violence and the storms of life.

I am reminded of the church lady who was told she only had a few weeks to live. She called her pastor over, and together they made plans for her funeral: what dress to wear, what pallbearers, even what songs to sing and scriptures to read. Then, she arranged for something odd: "Be sure to bury me with my Bible in one hand and a fork in the other."

"What for?" asked the pastor.

The lady explained that she had been to innumerable church suppers, and whenever they took her plate, they asked her to keep her fork because there would be dessert.

"So, when they all ask about the fork, tell them that this Christian knew—THE BEST IS YET TO COME!"

PRAYER AND CRISIS

When Larry Gene Ashbrook entered our church building the night of September 15, 1999, he approached our custodian, Jeff Laster, and asked, "Where's that #$@%! Prayer Meeting?" He did not ask for the Pastor or the Youth Rally...or the Treasurer's office.

He asked for directions to the Prayer Meeting.

The target of his evil intentions was intended to be the intercessors. That is the ministry he originally wanted to thwart. Normally, prayer meeting would have been held in the sanctuary, but because of the "Saw You at the Pole" rally, the weekly prayer meeting had been moved to the Fellowship Hall.

What role does prayer have to play in the face of traumatic crisis and its aftermath? The older I get, the more convinced I am of the critical place that prayer has in the life of the individual believer and in the Kingdom of God generally.

Prayer

Everyone prays.

In Nepal, Buddhists place written prayers inside metal cylinders and spin them. Each time the cylinder rotates, they believe a prayer goes up to the universe (Samsara). Some tech-savvy Buddhists download their prayers onto their computer hard drives that spin at 5,400 revolutions per minute!

In Japan, well-dressed businessmen will visit a Shinto shrine and pay a minimum of $50 for a priest to offer prayer on their behalf. The priest will bang a drum to get their god's attention and then say a prayer.

In Taiwan, truck drivers will litter the highways with cheap false "money" to appease the ghosts of the road and protect their rigs.

Hindus seek to appease their myriads of gods and spirits with food, flowers, and animal sacrifices.

Jews will stuff written prayers in the cracks of the Wailing Wall at the Temple Mount in Jerusalem.

Even Atheists pray! Back in the heyday of Communism, Russian citizens would have a "red corner" in their homes where ancient icons were replaced with pictures of Lenin, and the national newspaper, *Pravda*, would urge them to "think of Stalin" when they needed help or direction.

Americans and Prayer

In America, students used to intone, "God is great. God is good. Let us thank Him for this food." In spite of the fact that the Supreme Court has declared public prayers in schools unconstitutional, 45 percent of Americans (55 percent of Christians) still pray on a daily basis.[19] As long as there are math tests, students will pray silently, no matter what the Supreme Court says.

I was urged to write a chapter on the role of prayer in terms of crisis. Although the need for such was immediately obvious, I write with great reluctance. I am absolutely convinced we could not have survived our catastrophe without prayer, our own and those on our behalf. I am confident that for several months, at least, Wedgwood was the most prayed-for church in the world.

It was prayer that provided protection for us during the disaster and that kept the destruction to a minimum. It was prayer that sustained us after the shooting, drawing us closer to one another and closer to God so that what the enemy meant for our destruction, God worked for our good (Romans 8:28).

---

[19] https://www.pewresearch.org/fact-tank/2016/05/04/5-facts-about-prayer/

Yet, still, I realize that my own prayer life is woefully lacking. I am a "Type A," action-oriented doer personality. If hard work could bring in the Kingdom, people like me would have done so decades ago.

I have many questions about prayer, questions both theological and personal that hinder my passion and persistency in prayer.

But, through the years, I have come to realize what John Bunyan, author of *The Pilgrim's Progress*, has well said:

"You can do no more than pray, after you have prayed, but you cannot do more than pray UNTIL you have prayed" (all caps added for emphasis).

For more than 30 years of ministry, I have had pinned to the bookshelf across from my desk the constant reminder:

"When we work, *we* work.
When we pray, *God* works."

The Church in America is adept at organization, marketing, and promotion but, for the most part, is spiritually anemic. There is a story of a Chinese pastor who was brought to the United States to observe the Kingdom there. He was shown mega-church facilities, radio and TV stations, publishing houses, contemporary Christian music, and so forth. When he got back to China (where there are now more than 100 million believers willing to pay with their lives or their freedom for their faith), he told his brothers, "It is utterly astonishing what American churches have accomplished without God."

Americans are, on the whole, too self-sufficient and too prosperous to be great prayer warriors. Too many of us tend to think of prayer as something to be involved with only when we are desperate and there is nothing left to do. It is like a football game when the home team is losing, time is running out, and the quarterback heaves the ball desperately downfield, hoping for a last-second miracle catch. Roger Staubach of the Dallas Cowboys called it a "Hail Mary" pass after a common Catholic prayer.

Someone has well said, "Only he who is helpless can truly pray."

Almost from birth, we aspire to self-reliance. It is a celebrated triumph every time a young child learns to do something for himself: using the bathroom, tying his shoes, buttoning his shirt, or riding a bike.

"I do it myself!" cries the defiant two-year-old.

As adults, we pridefully pay our own way, deriding those who need help from the government. When faced with challenges, we turn to self-help books that line the shelves in drugstores and airport bookstores.

The truth is, as Jesus tells us, "Without Me you can do nothing" (John 15:5).

Jesus' Prayer Life

Jesus prayed when His life was busy and crowded. As He was sought after by miracle-seeking throngs, it was His practice to rise before dawn and retreat to a secret place alone to pray (Mark 1:35).

When He had important decisions to make, Jesus sought His Father. Before choosing the 12 disciples into whom He would pour His life and to whom He would entrust the Kingdom, Jesus spent the whole night in prayer on the mountain (Luke 6:12-13).

Jesus prayed when He suffered from grief and sadness. After hearing that Herod had cruelly beheaded His cousin, John the Baptist, Jesus tried to withdraw to a secluded place in prayer (Matthew 14:13).

When He was concerned about people He loved, Jesus prayed. In the upper room, He told Simon, who would soon betray Him in His greatest time of need, that "Satan has demanded permission to sift you like wheat; but I have prayed for you" (Luke 22:31-32).

Finally, Jesus prayed agonizingly during His darkest trial, alone in the Garden of Gethsemane (Luke 22:39-46).

Every temptation Jesus endured, He did so through the indwelling power of the Holy Spirit, activated by His prayerful reliance on the Father.

Every miracle He accomplished was due to His constant, reliance on His Heavenly Father through prayer. Constant abiding and depending through prayer was the key to Jesus' life and ministry.

The Saints and the Necessity of Prayer

Virtually anybody throughout Church history who ever accomplished anything for the Kingdom gives testimony to the centrality of Prayer for Christian life and growth.

Martin Luther—The progenitor of the Protestant Reformation who prayed three hours a day said, "He that has prayed well has studied well."

John Wesley—This spiritual Father of Methodism who travelled across Britain and the American colonies insisted, "God does nothing but in answer to prayer."

John Calvin—The Geneva reformer whose *Institutes* is the foundation of reformed theology declared, "Words fail to express how necessary prayer is."

William Cowper—This hymn writer wrote, "Satan trembles when he sees the weakest saint upon his knees."

William Carey—The Father of Modern Missions said, "Prayer—secret, fervent, believing prayer—lies at the root of all personal godliness."

Thomas Hooker—This American Puritan claimed, "Prayer is my life work, and it is by means of it that I carry on the rest."

J. Hudson Taylor—The founder of the China Inland Mission had hour-long prayer times at 6 am, noon, 3 pm, 9 pm, and midnight. He maintained his mission without asking anyone but God for financial support.

Charles Haddon Spurgeon—The greatest preacher of the Victorian Era taught his people to pray heartfelt, passionate prayers. When asked the secret to his success, he simply replied, "My people pray for me." When someone asked him about the power source for his magnificent tabernacle, Spurgeon took him to the basement where hundreds of intercessors were on their knees in prayer.

Can all these giants of the faith be mistaken? Why are we so resistant in this matter of prayer? Peter Wagner surveyed nearly 600 pastors about their prayer life. He found that mainline denominational pastors averaged 22 minutes a day in prayer.[20] Pentecostal pastors spend more time in prayer a day than average.[21] It is no coincidence that the worldwide growth of Pentecostalism has been phenomenal in recent years. In 1970, Pentecostals numbered 74.5 million; by 2000, they had grown to nearly 482 million. The Global Evangelization Movement predicts that by 2025, there will be 740 million Pentecostals worldwide.[22] Of the world's largest 20 churches, five are Pentecostal.[23]

Korean Prayer Power

I am amazed when I hear of the amazing growth of Christianity in South Korea. Today, approximately one-third of the entire population claims to be

---

[20] C. Peter Wagner, *Prayer Shield: How to Intercede for Pastors. Christian Leaders and Others on the Spiritual Frontlines* (Ventura: Regal Books, 1992), p. 79.

[21] http://www.bpnews.net/20918/most-pastors-unsatisfied-with-their-personal-prayer-lives

[22] http://pneumareview.com/worldwide-growth-of-pentecostals-and-charismatics/

[23] https://leadnet.org/world/

evangelical Christians. The unique distinction of Korean Christians is their emphasis on concerted prayer.

Virtually every church holds a pre-dawn prayer meeting every day of the year! Senior pastors lead these because they insist, "That is where the power is."

A majority of Korean churches regularly schedule all-night prayer vigils on Friday nights. Others do the same on Wednesday evenings. Nearly half of Korean pastors spend at least two hours a day in prayer.

More than 100 churches have purchased "Prayer Mountains" that serve as prayer and fasting retreat centers. One prayer mountain receives about 750,000 visits a year.

Peter Wagner visited Seoul, and there he met with Sundo Kim, Pastor of Kwanglim Methodist Church. They were in the midst of a 40-day prayer emphasis, meeting every morning at 5 am. Wagner asked if he could come and was warmly invited.

That night, a typhoon hit the city. Sixty lives were lost in the flooding. At 5 am, the winds were still blowing at 75 mph. As Wagner took a taxi to the church, he wondered who would *walk* to church in weather like that. When he arrived, he was astounded to find the sanctuary filled with 4,000 prayer warriors, and if a seat had not been reserved for him, Wagner would have had to stand with many others!

Prayer at Wedgwood

I had grown increasingly convinced of the necessity of prayer in my ministry at Wedgwood. With this in mind, I established a Thursday morning prayer watch at 6 am. Then, we held the same on Sunday mornings at 6 am. While the attendees were not huge in number, they were faithful. Wednesday evening prayer meeting has always been a staple at Wedgwood.

Later, we established a "Watchman on the Wall" prayer ministry where we invited people to sign up for 60-minute periods of prayer around the clock. We kept track of prayer requests and answers to prayer through the dedicated labors of my Administrative Assistant, Debbie Gillette. We advertised a prayer "hot line" and got many requests from around the nation and the world. Scores of missionaries sent out from Wedgwood would send us their prayer needs.

We encouraged every member to have at least one "Prayer Partner" with whom they could intercede together. I have led a Tuesday morning 6 am prayer fellowship at a local restaurant the entirety of my ministry. Several other prayer groups would meet weekly as well.

As feeble as these efforts might appear compared to our Chinese and Korean brethren, I am convinced this prayer emphasis at Wedgwood was the primary factor that helped mitigate against the evil effects of that tragic September evening in 1999.

Whereas other churches might fall to pieces and die due to such traumatic circumstances, we drew closer, and we actually grew in the subsequent years. If you are seeking solutions to the problem of church security, my advice is to begin with emphasizing the critical need for prayer.

The Sunday after the shooting, a sister church from Tulsa, Oklahoma, sent a van of Intercessors to prayer walk around our property all morning long. I look forward to meeting those prayer warriors someday, if only in Heaven.

At 6 am that Sunday, hundreds of folks showed up for prayer watch in the sanctuary. The atmosphere was electric!

As I have stated previously, we received about 20,000 emails and letters from believers around the world during the next several weeks, encouraging us, assuring us of their prayer and support. We lined the walls of the hallways in our building so that members could read them and sense the support the body of Christ was giving us during those months of grief and sorrow.

Does Prayer Work?

In Somerset Maugham's novel, *Of Human Bondage*, the main character is a young boy who was born with a physical affliction then called "clubfoot." In child-like faith, he decided to assault the Throne of Heaven to plead with God to miraculously heal his infirmity. For days, he pled with the Father for mercy. Finally, he went to bed one night, completely confident the Great Physician would answer his heartfelt cries by the morning. He could hardly sleep, and when the morning finally arrived, he jumped joyfully out of bed only to fall flat on his face due to his deformed foot that still could not support his weight. From that moment, the character, like Maugham, became an atheist.

Anyone who has walked with God for any length of time has experienced the disappointment of seemingly unanswered prayer. It is important to remember that God always responds to the prayers of His children. Sometimes He says, "Yes," to our request; sometimes He says, "Not yet"; and, at times, His answer is simply, "No."

There are many "unanswered" prayers in the Bible where God refused the requests of the petitioner. We have already noted the prayers of Moses, Elijah, and Jonah when they asked the Almighty to take their lives. Thankfully, God denied those pleas. David asked for the right to build God's temple, and Jehovah said, "No." Peter suggested on the Mount of Transfiguration that he and his friends build a shrine there, and Jesus simply ignored him. Paul pled with God three times to remove his "thorn in the flesh," and God refused, saying, "My grace is sufficient for you" (2 Corinthians 12:9).

Even Jesus Christ, God's only Son, was denied when He pled with the Father, "Let this cup pass from Me!" (Matthew 26:39). Are you not glad the Father refused?

Does prayer "work," or is it just "coincidence" when our petitions seem to be granted? William Temple once said, "When I pray, coincidences happen, and when I don't, they don't."

Once again in this issue of prayer, the mysteries of God's immutable sovereignty and human responsibility seem to clash. But, both truths are laid out in God's Word.

In Ezekiel 36:36, God speaks of His sovereign power: "I, the Lord, have spoken and I will do it." Period. God will do what He determines to do.

Yet, in the very next verse, God says, "I will also let the house of Israel inquire of Me to do this for them." God seems to move in accordance to our supplications to Him.

I do not understand all of the mystery here, but I agree with Jack Hayford, who observed about prayer, "If we don't, He won't."

Examples of Powerful Prayer

One of the great historical events of our lifetime has been the unexpected "fall" of the Soviet Empire. No one saw this coming when it happened in the late 1980s. It caught all our intelligence agencies by surprise.

Peter Wagner, in his book, *Churches That Pray*, tells the story of Mark Geppert who spent two weeks in the Soviet Union to do nothing but pray. His last four days were spent in Kiev, the capital of Ukraine, near the infamous Chernobyl nuclear power plant.

On the morning of his last day, April 25, 1986, Geppert went to the town square, sat on a bench under a statue of Lenin, and prayed. Every 15 minutes, the town clock would chime, and he would renew his prayers.

Just before noon, he felt a release in his spirit. He sensed that God was starting a work that would break the stronghold of Communism. He was led in his spirit to praise God out loud. Shaking his fist at the statue, he shouted, "Lenin, you're history!" Then, he asked God to give him a sign of confirmation. Just then, the hands of the clock reached noon...silence! The chimes failed to ring out!

That was the exact time when mistakes were made that led to the nuclear disaster at Chernobyl some 12 hours later. Many observers believe this disaster to be the climax of technical chaos that led to the fall of Communism and the break-up of the Soviet Union.

On a more personal level, my wife, Kay, came from a family of nonbelievers who were somewhat nonplussed when their youngest daughter married a man who was preparing to be a Baptist pastor. It seemed that the more she tried to talk to them about her faith, the more they shut down in their spirit. All we could do was pray. Then, after several decades, her eldest sister was born again. Encouraged by this answer to prayer, we kept on praying for the rest of the family.

Finally, after 26 years of intercession, her father gave his life to Christ. Several weeks later, I had the privilege of baptizing my 74-year-old father-in-law.

When You Cannot Pray

For many Christians, especially after dark, traumatic experiences, there comes a time the saints call "The Dark Night of the Soul," when one simply cannot pray. The soul is so wounded that the words will not come.

After the shooting, my wife was so emotionally and spiritually numb, she just could not pray. Her mind could not focus; her heart ached too much. This condition lasted for weeks, even months.

The Word of God acknowledges this reality. In Romans 8:26, we read:

"In the same way the Spirit also helps our weakness; for we do not know how to pray as we should, but the Spirit Himself intercedes for us with groanings too deep for words."

It is when we cannot pray, when our hearts are too broken and our minds are too confused to pray, that the intercession of others sustains us.

First of all, we read that the Holy Spirit intercedes on our behalf. In verse 27 of the previous passage, we are told that the Holy Spirit "intercedes for the saints according to the will of God."

Secondly, one of the High Priestly ministries of the risen Christ is intercession for the saints (Hebrews 7:25). Think of it—Jesus Christ Himself is our personal Intercessor before the Throne of the Father!

Finally, Christians have the God-given responsibility of praying for one another. We are instructed to pray for each other's healing (James 5:13-16), for open doors of ministry (Ephesians 6:19), for peace (Philippians 4:6-7), and, as part of our armor, against the schemes of Satan (Ephesians 6:18).

How to Prepare

Of all the steps that might be taken to prepare for traumatic disaster that might befall you, your family, or your organization, the most effective by far is the preparation of prayer. Be a man or woman of prayer. Be a praying church. Put on the divine defense and protection that can only be ascertained by prayerful intercession.

Prayer is much like athletic competition. In order to win the game on Friday night, it takes weeks of practice, wind sprints, grass drills, and scrimmages when no one is in the stands cheering you on. The decision to win is the decision to *prepare* to win.

Some people mistakenly believe that all true prayer with Almighty God should be spontaneous and spectacular. On the contrary, far more often it involves dedication and discipline. Much can be said for the blue-collar, lunch-bucket, and vanilla-flavored, day-in-and-day-out prayer. The earth may not move, lightning may not flash, but, over time, the still small voice of God can be discerned, and we are transformed.

And when the "evil day" comes, we are not blown out of the water.

Amen. So be it.

THE BLESSING OF BROKENNESS

Have you heard about the thieves who broke into the department store one night...and did not steal a thing? All they did was SWITCH THE PRICE TAGS!

Flat screen televisions went for 99 cents. Shoelaces were marked at $6.99. Couches were priced at $2.99 while ties were listed at $1,599!

Part of the uniqueness of Jesus Christ was the way He overturned the values of His day...and ours. Our culture says, "Look out for number one." Jesus said, "The first shall be last" (Matthew 20:16). The world insists, "Winning isn't everything; it's the ONLY thing!" Jesus told us, "For whoever wishes to save his life will lose it" (Matthew 16:25).

Society says, "He who dies with the most toys wins." Jesus says, "For what does it profit a man if he gains the whole world and loses or forfeits himself?" (Matthew 16:26).

Jesus' radical revolution in values is shocking at times!

- We only truly live when we die.
- We conquer by losing.
- The greatest of all must be the servant to all.
- Blessed are the poor...the mourners...the meek...the hungry...the persecuted!

Truly, Jesus SWITCHED THE PRICE TAGS OF LIFE!

When Catastrophe Strikes

When disasters occur in our lives, they leave us devastated, shaken, and broken. The Law of Karma begs the question, "What did I do to deserve this? What is wrong with me?" We wonder if we will ever recover.

The Bible is filled, both Old and New Testaments, with the paradoxical truths that our sovereign God is especially near to those with broken hearts.

Isaiah 57:15—"For thus says the High and Lofty One Who inhabits eternity, whose name is Holy: 'I dwell in the high and holy place, With him who has a contrite and humble spirit, To revive the spirit of the humble, And to revive the heart of the contrite ones.'"

Psalm 34:18—"The Lord is near to those who have a broken heart, And saves such as have a contrite spirit."

Psalm 51:17—"The sacrifices of God are a broken spirit, A broken and a contrite heart—These, O God, You will not despise."

Proverbs 3:34 and 1 Peter 5:5—"God resists the proud, But gives grace to the humble."

In the parable of the Publican (tax collector) and the Pharisee found in Luke 18, it was the humble, broken Publican, who could not even lift his eyes to Heaven as he begged for mercy, who went away justified. The proud, self righteous Pharisee left the temple still in his sins.

The Roman Empire of Jesus' day did not consider humility a virtue. One openly paraded his status, if he had any at all. The Greco-Roman world organized itself the way most airlines do: first-class passengers board first, s in better seats, and are served with fine china and silver.

Cicero wrote, "Rank must be preserved." Roman society had the Emperor and 600 senators at the top. Then came the Equestrians, citizens, non-citizens, and, lastly, slaves.

So, when Paul opened his letter to the Romans as "a slave of Christ Jesus," he was committing social suicide! And what can be said of Jesus, who was described as "a friend of sinners"? Who died a death designed only for criminal slaves? Who essentially said that the greatest of all is the slave of all (Mark 10:44)?

When Jesus stated in the Sermon on the Mount, "Blessed are the meek, For they shall inherit the earth" (Matthew 5:5), He was not extolling a shy, self-effacing, false humility like Uriah Heep in Charles Dickens' *David Copperfield* ("I'm just your 'umble servant...").

The term *meek* in the Beatitudes means "power under control." The picture is that of a wild mustang running aimlessly across the plains. First, it must be lassoed by the cowboy and then taken to the corral to be fitted with a bit and bridle. Then, a saddle is placed on its back, and finally, a broncobuster mounts it and hangs on until the horse realizes all the bucking he can manage is useless. He finally submits to the cowboy.

Westerners say that the horse has been "broken."

The horse has not lost one iota of its power, but now its strength and energy can serve a useful purpose.

I would submit to you, dear reader, that the catastrophes in our lives serve the purpose of Almighty God to "break" us so that He might use us as He desires.

In fact, I would say *God only truly uses broken people and broken things*.

The lad's lunch of five loaves and two fish was hopelessly unable to feed the masses until Jesus blessed it and *broke* it.

The potter is unable to fashion the jar into something beautiful until the clay is *broken* and the lumps are removed.

The Example of Moses

Two prime examples from God's Word stand out to me as illustrations of the Blessing of Brokenness.

The first is that of Moses. Miraculously rescued by Pharaoh's daughter from the bulrushes of the Nile, Moses was raised in the royal palace. He had the best education in the highest culture of his day. Some contend he was being groomed to become the next Pharaoh. Acts 7:22 describes Moses as "learned in all the wisdom of the Egyptians, and was mighty in words and deeds."

At the prime age of 40, Moses answered God's call to give his life to the liberation of his people, the Israelite slaves. Confident and full of himself, he intervened on behalf of a slave being beaten by an Egyptian taskmaster and killed the perpetrator.

"One down, 9,999,999 to go!"

But instead of being praised for his courageous act of liberation, he is suspected and resisted by his chosen countrymen and wanted "Dead or Alive" by the Egyptian officials.

The only thing to do was run for his life! And so, like a whipped puppy with his tail between his legs, he winds up in the Midian desert—alone, defeated, and dejected.

When the story picks up again, Moses is living with his father-in-law, Jethro, tending his sheep. He has lost it all. His reputation is shattered; his education is useless; he has nothing left to call his own. He is eating at Jethro's table, tending Jethro's sheep, wearing Jethro's hand-me-down clothes, and sleeping in Jethro's tent.

Moses is 80 years old now...not exactly in his prime.

In short, Moses is *broken*.

Now he is almost useable for God.

Almost. He still has one thing he can call his own: his rod. And so, from the Burning Bush, the voice of the God of Abraham, Isaac, and Jacob calls out to Moses and asks, "What is that in your hand?" (Exodus 4:2).

"A rod," Moses replies. And not just a rod, but *his* rod—his defense, his support among the desert rocks and gullies, his hope and security.

And God instructs Moses, "Throw it down."

Now, at last, at 80 years of age, Moses is truly *broken*. Now he is useable to God. His rod has become the Rod of God. With God's Rod, he can turn the Nile to blood, bring in and dissipate lice, locusts, flies, and hail. With the Rod of God, Moses can part the Red Sea for his people's deliverance and close it up again to swallow Pharaoh and his army.

With the Rod of God, Moses brings water from the rock and victory over enemies.

But nothing happened until Moses was broken because *God only uses broken people and broken things.*

The Example of Paul

From the New Testament comes the story of the Apostle Paul, the greatest and most gifted saint in Church history.

But he did not start out that way.

Saul of Tarsus, as he was originally known, was one of the brightest and best of young Jewish scholars of his day. Born into a Jewish family of the tribe of Benjamin in the city of Tarsus, he soon went to Jerusalem for his education. A "Pharisee of the Pharisees," as he described himself, he was accepted into the most exclusive sect of Judaism. His personal tutor was Gamaliel, one of the leading Jewish scholars in the entire world.

As a young zealot, Saul was central in the effort to purge Judaism of the radical new sect, which would later be known as Christianity. As the first martyr, Stephen, was being stoned to death, it was Saul who held the cloaks and encouraged the executioners.

It was Saul who was charged with the task of eradicating these heretical Christians in Damascus, to which many had fled. On the way, he was confronted with a vision of God, who upbraided him for attacking His very own.

Immediately converted to the Faith, Saul was charged by God with ministry to the Gentiles. One would have thought, on the contrary, that he would have been perfectly suited to minister to his fellow Jews.

And this is how he began his ministry: contending, debating with the great scholars in the synagogue in Damascus over the claims of Jesus being the Messiah. No one could hold his own with this young protagonist. However, instead of revival, contention and strife resulted, so much so that a number of his enemies swore they would assassinate him in the gate of the city.

Having discovered the plot, his friends spirited him out of the metropolis by lowering him in a basket over the city wall. Could anything have been more humiliating for this young and brilliant disciple? Lowered in a basket and running for his life! In a word: *broken*.

Hold that thought.

Saul immediately journeyed to Jerusalem where the Apostles met him with suspicion, but Barnabas recognized his sincerity and stood up on his behalf

There again, he went into the Temple to debate the greatest Jewish minds in the world. Once again, he was successful as a debater but a failure as a missionary. The resulting riot was so egregious that the Apostles gave him a one-way ticket out of town.

Worst of all, the result of Saul's banishment was a revival in Jerusalem, especially among the priests!

And so, young Saul returned to his home in Tarsus. There he lived at home, working in his father's shop—a first century "slacker"—for 10 years!

After 10 years of failure and loneliness there in Tarsus, a revival broke out in the city of Antioch. The Apostles had sent Barnabas to check things out, and he soon found the task bigger than he could manage by himself. So, remembering the gifted Saul of Tarsus, Barnabas brought him to assist in the discipling of all these new converts. And, when God called the church there to send forth missionaries to the Gentiles, it fell to Barnabas and Saul to answer the call.

The rest, as they say, is history. Saul took the name "Paul," and he became the pre-eminent church planter of the first century as well as the author of nearly half of the New Testament through his theologically rich letters to the churches.

Years later, the Corinthian church that Paul had started was being torn apart by factions, each harking to their favorite leaders: Peter, Apollos, and Paul himself. His supporters had written to him to ask him to update his resume, brag on himself a bit to make their case stronger.

Though Paul had much he could have boasted about to enhance his authority, he refused to do it. Instead, he said, "If I have to boast, I will boast of what pertains to my *weakness*" (2 Corinthians 11:30, emphasis mine).

Then, he makes the strangest claim. It is so paradoxical that Paul fears they may not believe him, so he makes a solemn vow to God. The high point, the pinnacle of his career, was that humiliating day when he was let down in a basket at Damascus in order to flee for his life. That ignominious day was the beginning of the Breaking Process as God prepared to make this proud, brilliant, self-sufficient scholar of Judaism into His Missionary to the Gentiles.

Paul goes on to tell us that God had revealed to him that His divine power is "made perfect in weakness" (12:9).

Then, he goes on to say, "...most gladly I will rather boast in my infirmities, that the power of Christ may rest upon me...For when I am weak, then I am strong" (12:9-10).

God only uses the weak...the *broken*.

The Problem with Pride

God has insisted He will not share His glory with any person. That is why He has chosen the foolish, the weak things, and people of this world to carry out His purposes. God chooses a washed-up octogenarian to defeat mighty Pharaoh and deliver His people from bondage. He chooses a humble shepherd boy to defeat the giant, Goliath, and lead His people to victory. God uses the muddy Jordan River to wash away Naaman's leprosy. He drafts a ragtag bunch of losers and slow learners to be the foundation of His Kingdom.

As Paul himself summarizes,

"But God has chosen the foolish things of the world to put to shame the wise, and God has chosen the weak things of the world to put to shame the things which are mighty...that no flesh should glory in His presence" (Corinthians 1:27, 29).

Jacob and Esau

God makes the strange statement in both the Old Testament (Malachi 1:2 3) and the New Testament (Romans 9:13), that "Jacob have I loved, but Esa have I hated."

What is that about?

Jacob and Esau, you will remember, were the twin sons of Isaac and Rebekah. Esau was his father's favorite: strong, ruddy, a hunter, and self-sufficient. Jacob, on the other hand, was his mother's pet: relatively weak and having to rely on his own wits as opposed to his brother's strength. As such, Jacob tricked his older brother out of his birthright and his father's blessing as the firstborn son and then had to run for his life to far off Haran to live with his Uncle Laban.

Esau is the epitome of self-sufficiency, hubris, and human pride, all of which God hates and sets Himself up against.

Jacob, meanwhile, has to undergo the Breaking Process. Tricked by his Uncle Laban out of 14 years of hard labor in order to win his wife, Rachel, Jacob finally tries to return home again to face the music and the vengeance of his brother Esau.

The night before that fateful meeting, Jacob wrestles with The Angel of the Lord (Christ Himself) all night long. In the process, his hip becomes dislocated, and he cannot even stand on his own. Utterly *broken*, Jacob clings to God for life and in the process is so changed that God gives him a new name. Instead of Jacob "the schemer," he will be known as Israel "the prince of God." He will be the patriarch through whose lineage the Messiah will eventually come.

Because *God only uses broken people and broken things*.

The Great Sin

C.S. Lewis, in his classic book, *Mere Christianity*, has a chapter entitled, "The Great Sin." In it, he makes the claim that the greatest sin of all is not some vile sin of the flesh nor a wicked murder or lustful act. To Lewis, the greatest sin of all is Pride.

It is pride that keeps man from trusting in God's grace. It was pride that kept the Prodigal son in the pigpen of life for so long. It was pride that caused Adam and Eve to rebel in Eden ("You will be like God" from Genesis 3:5). It was pride that caused Lucifer, the Shining One, to become the devil himself.

Thus, ever and always, "God resists the proud but gives grace to the humble" (1 Peter 5:5).

Salvation itself is "by grace...that not of yourselves; it is the gift of God, not of works, *lest anyone should boast*" (Ephesians 2:8-9, emphasis mine).

God's Mission Statement

It has become a common practice for businesses, organizations, and even individuals to map out a Mission Statement to explain and clarify one's purposes and goals. Just what are we all about? What values guide our decisions and actions?

As Jesus first spoke in public in the synagogue beginning His ministry, He quoted Isaiah 61 and gave His/God's Mission Statement:

"The Spirit of the Lord is upon Me,
Because He has anointed Me
To preach the gospel to the POOR;
He has sent Me to heal the BROKENHEARTED,
To proclaim liberty to the CAPTIVES,
And recovery of sight to the BLIND,
To set at liberty those who are OPPRESSED" (Luke 4:18, emphasis mine)

It is rather hard to miss it. Jesus is clear that the Good News of the Kingdom is for the benefit of the *Broken*: the poor, the brokenhearted, the captives, the blind, and the oppressed.

It was the broken, ragamuffin, abused, and oppressed who were most drawn to Jesus. It was the proud, self-righteous, well-off, and self-sufficient who were Jesus' worst critics and chief opponents.

In Isaiah 61:3, the prophet goes on to explain that when Messiah comes, He will:

"...grant those who mourn in Zion,
Giving them a garland instead of ashes,
The oil of gladness instead of mourning,
The mantle of praise instead of a spirit of fainting.
So they will be called oaks of righteousness,
The planting of the Lord, that He may be glorified."

That fateful evening of September 15, 1999, our sovereign God allowed a crazed madman to enter our church, snuff out the lives of seven of our brightest and best, and traumatize many of His followers through unmitigated terror and violence.

We were, and still are, a church of *broken* people. But that is precisely the kind of people God specializes in using for His glory.

In fact, *God only uses broken people and broken things.*

CONCLUSION

An ancient Chinese parable tells of a man who bought a pony for his son. "That's good!" exclaimed his friends. But the pony ran away. "That's bad," said his neighbors. However, the pony returned with 12 wild mustangs with him. "Wonderful!" said his friends. Then, as the son was training one of the wild ponies, he fell and broke his leg. "That's terrible!" said the neighbors. Soon, the local warlord came through the village conscripting all the young men for war. Fortunately, the man's son was spared because of his broken leg.

The point of the story is clear: We are not always wise enough to discern what is good or bad.

Religious Response to Pain

As was discussed in an earlier chapter, all the great religions of the world are forced to address the problem of Evil. Why do innocent people suffer so?

Buddhism frankly admits that suffering is a universal element of the human condition. The answer to it is to learn to live without any desire whatsoever. When you achieve a state of total indifference, suffering will have lost its hold on you.

Islam also recognizes the fact of human suffering. Their answer is for one to submit to the will of Allah. Muslim parents grieve deeply at the death of a child, but they do not protest against Allah.

Hinduism contends that human suffering is the just and right punishment for sins in previous lives. It is the Law of Karma.

Secular Government, especially in the West, valiantly tries to eliminate the pain and suffering of its citizens by vast spending for education, funds for scientific and medical research, dams, roads, water projects, and so forth. But, in spite of billions spent on technological advances, there seems to be more pain and suffering than ever! The latest statistics tell us that an estimated 1.4 million Americans attempt suicide each year.[24] Approximately 1.1 million of those are teenagers.[25]

Christianity teaches that pain and suffering are inescapable in this sin-stricken world. One day, God Himself will heal the planet of all pain, sickness, sorrow, and death. In the meantime, He uses trials to refine His people.

God does not alleviate all pain and suffering in this world, but He brings good from the evil that abounds. As Romans 8:28 boldly declares, "...all things work together for good for those who love God...."

In 1850, an ambitious dry goods dealer emigrated from Bavaria to California. Unfortunately, during a storm, he lost all his goods and materials as the hold had to be lightened to save the ship.

In a feeble effort to reimburse him, the captain gave him bolts of sail canvas, and then bade him good day as he embarked in San Francisco. Trying to make the best of a bad situation, the man tried to make slacks out of the sail canvas. To his dismay, he discovered he had no thread left to sew on pockets. In desperation, he went to a blacksmith and had them riveted on.

The rugged sailcloth slacks became a hit among the gold miners, who needed durable cloth that lasted. Soon, the merchant had all the orders he could handle.

His name? Levi Strauss, the originator of Levi jeans.

---

[24] https://afsp.org/about-suicide/suicide-statistics/

[25] http://prp.jasonfoundation.com/facts/youth-suicide-statistics/

Good from Bad at Wedgwood

One of the truly good results from the Wedgwood tragedy was a new and strengthened sense of unity in the church. In the immediate aftermath, the members clung together as never before. Lukewarm members became faithful and involved. Criticism and grumbling ceased. Services were packed. Worship was exhilarating!

Nothing unites us like a common enemy.

The body of Christ in Fort Worth grew together. Altamesa Church of Christ and Wedgwood Baptist Church became sister churches. Community services were packed out as choirs joined together and pulpits were exchanged.

One of the positive outcomes of this new sense of unity was the birth of what came to be known as Tarrant Net. Led by eventual Director, Jeff Sanders, evangelicals of various denominations and ministries joined together for monthly lunches where we got to hear each other's hearts and pray and worship together. We joined hands for "Convoy of Hope" ministry in the inner city and partnered with local schools for "Read to Win" literacy tutoring. This fellowship crossed both racial and denominational lines.

The city of Fort Worth soon recognized the great need for coordination in the mental health community. It is a known fact that the state of Texas is among the lowest per capita in spending on mental health. Tarrant County is among the lowest in the state in allocations for those needs.

Led by then State Representative, Mike Moncrief, later to become the mayor of Fort Worth, leaders in the mental health sector got together to streamline public response to psychological emergencies, treating childhood, adolescent, and adult cases via a central clearing house called the Mental Health Connection. This coordinative effort became a model for communities around the nation and was rewarded with hundreds of thousands of dollars in federal grants.

The Bullet in the Hymnal

Perhaps more than anything, we came to realize just how critical an understanding of and appreciation for the sovereignty of God is as we make our way through the storms of life.

Police Officer Chip Gillette, also a member of Wedgwood, was the first law enforcement officer to enter the worship center in the minutes after the shooting started. He opened the sanctuary door just as the shooter took his own life.

In the following hours, ATF and Fort Worth Police swarmed the building, investigating the horrors that had taken place. Chip was there until late in the evening, surveying the chaos. Bodies on the floor, blood stains on the carpet, bomb shards scattered all around, and bullet holes in the sheetrock as well as the smell of cordite all assaulted his senses like an emotional tsunami. He decided he had had enough and decided to go home.

Through the night, his soul was in anguish as he questioned God, "Why wasn't I there?"

By morning, Chip finally felt that God had spoken to him, saying, "Go back to the church...I have something for you."

Entering the worship center, he once again felt the heartache of his sanctuary becoming a killing field. The place where he had repeatedly experienced the palpable presence of God was now desecrated by insane violence and death.

He walked up and down the aisles that morning, looking at every pew and asking God why He wanted him there again. By that time, the bodies were gone, and the shell casings and shrapnel were cleared away.

As he tearfully made his way up the aisle, he noticed a bullet hole in the edge of a pew. The course of the bullet led his eyes to a hymnal that was askew in the rack. When he picked up the hymnal, he realized that one of the gunman's bullets was lodged in the songbook. The book fell open in his hands, right where the bullet had spent itself on the page where Handel's "Hallelujah Chorus" was found. The bullet pointed to the words:

"King of kings, and Lord of lords,
and He shall reign for ever and ever."

At that moment, God answered Chip's question, "Why wasn't I there?" God was there.

He was reigning, even on that fateful night at Wedgwood.

He is reigning today in every corner of the Universe.

He shall be reigning...when every knee bows and every tongue confesses, "Jesus is Lord!"

Amen.

IMAGES OF HOPE AND HEALING

Pastor Al Meredith spoke hope and truth to the world. (Photo: James Morris)

Many gathered to worship and pray together at the TCU stadium. (Photo: James Morris)

The community showered Wedgwood with gifts and notes of encouragement. (Photo: James Morris)

Churches around the world were praying for Wedgwood.

Youth were allowed to write their thoughts on the concrete
where carpet had to be removed.

Wedgwood youth made scrapbook pages as a part of the healing process.

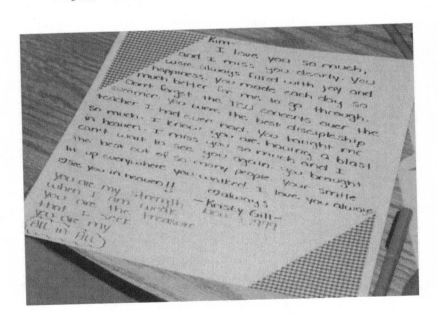

**Youth Minister Jay Fannin holds up the message
of truth that helped Wedgwood triumph
through the tragedy.**

This bear, after having been passed along by others who had experienced tragedy, was sent to Wedgwood to help bring comfort and healing.

(Photo: Michael Queen)

The hymn book found by Chip Gillette with God's profound message
of hope: "King of kings, and Lord of lords, and He shall reign for ever
and ever."

50111670R00095

Made in the USA
San Bernardino, CA
27 August 2019